GODS IN THE MAKING

*ESSAYS ON THE ROLE OF RELIGION
IN BRITAIN TODAY*

William Deller

Copyright © William Deller 2009

All rights reserved.

No part of this publication may be reproduced,
stored in a retrieval system, or transmitted
in any form or by any means, without
the prior permission in writing of the publisher,
nor be otherwise circulated in any form of binding or
cover other than that in which it is published and without
a similar condition including this condition being imposed
on the subsequent purchaser.

First published in Great Britain by Pen Press

All paper used in the printing of this book has been
made from wood grown in managed, sustainable forests.

ISBN13: 978-1-907172-28-1

Printed and bound in the UK
Pen Press is an imprint of Indepenpress Publishing Ltd
25 Eastern Place
Brighton BN2 1GJ

A catalogue record of this book is available from
the British Library

Cover design by Jacqueline Abromeit

In the attitude of silence the soul finds a clear path in a clearer light, and what is elusive and deceptive resolves itself into crystal clearness. Our life is a long and arduous quest after Truth.

Mahatma Gandhi

Where there is no religion, hypocrisy becomes good taste.

George Bernard Shaw

Contents

Preface	7
Introduction	9
Chapter	
1. Evolution	15
2. Sin and Society	23
3. Righteousness and Religion	40
4. Reincarnation	50
5. Orthodox Religion	59
6. False Gods	67
7. Righteousness in society	74
8. Religion for the Common Man	100
9. Conclusion	106
Further Reading	108

Preface

I make no claim to be expert in any of the topics addressed here. Rather, like the boy in the tale of the Emperor's new clothes, I point out that there is something odd going on. I make connections between various topics and demonstrate that those who claim to be authorities – whether in politics, finance, the media or the church – seem to be making a frightful mess of things. Much of the world seems to be travelling down an evolutionary road that leads nowhere. As always it is the common man, who is expected to defer to the experts, who suffers most.

An American Vice-President predicted in 1942 that the coming century would be the century of the common man. It is time the common man made it so, not by political revolution, but by calling for a religion that demands righteousness on the part of our leaders whatever position they occupy. Such a religion will be compatible with present scientific knowledge, and will include sanctions to encourage righteousness.

I make no claims of divine inspiration but rest my case on pragmatism; the pragmatism of evolution, of reincarnation, and of the common man who has to live day-by-day as best he can, utilizing whatever support he can find including God and righteousness. This book is a contribution to the ongoing debate on the part played by religion in our lives.

Introduction

Without God, there is no virtue, because there is no prompting of the conscience. Without God, we're mired in the material, that flat world that tells us only what the senses perceive. Without God, there is a coarsening of society. And without God, democracy will not and cannot long endure.

Ronald Reagan

It is difficult to exaggerate the extent and depth of the crises that threaten Britain. The media bombards us with news and opinions about the credit crunch, the banking crisis, the economic crisis. Because these are being acknowledged, however belatedly, at least the problems are being addressed. Nevertheless there are other, even more significant, crises that are being ignored. These include the spiritual, ethical, and moral crises that underlie and have contributed to the more obvious practical problems that presently occupy the attention of politicians and media. I believe that it is only by examining these areas of life that we can really get to grips with the more obvious material problems. These material crises, some of global proportions, are an early warning that mankind is travelling down an evolutionary blind alley that can end only in disaster.

The words of Ronald Reagan underline the importance of a belief in God for the life of a nation. In Britain this belief has become rather nominal; prayers are read at the beginning of Parliamentary sessions but then all thought of God and Godliness goes out of the window. The conduct of public affairs seems to take place in that flat world referred to by Reagan, with only the occasional reference to higher principles to gain some political advantage.

In Britain, Christianity – the national religion - is in decline and under attack. Church attendance is falling away. Simple religious principles seem to be less evident in the day-to-day lives of our communities and our institutions than they once were. Atheists deny the existence of God, sponsoring advertisements on London buses with the slogan "There's probably no God. Now stop worrying and enjoy your life", and books for children to warn them not to believe in God. A community nurse is suspended without pay because she offered to pray for a patient; this was said to demonstrate a lack of commitment to equality and diversity. A schoolgirl aged 5 is reprimanded by her teacher for talking about Jesus to another pupil.

There are various motivations for attempts to neuter the Christian religion: atheism, a misguided sense of fairness to other religions, a rejection of anything that cannot be explained in scientific terms, a reluctance to submit to a greater authority, or an aversion from anything that is part of British history. Nevertheless the overwhelming significance of a belief in God is conveyed by the words of Ronald Reagan; the Christian religion has been of primary importance throughout centuries of British history and the continuation of its central role is essential for the health of our society. Whatever benefit an individual gains from a faith in God, society derives a much greater benefit from the contribution such believers make. Faith is not just a matter of academic debate between atheists and believers; its beneficial effects permeate society.

However Christianity in Britain seems to accept a role of performing good works rather than playing a decisive part in influencing the essential quality of society. It seems to be squeezed between atheism – which wants no mention of spirituality – and Islam – which wants a unification of religion and state.

As a pragmatist I believe that a critical aspect of faith is its influence on the quality of life on earth. The hand of God, working through humans, can and should be expressed in personal life, at work, in civic affairs and in politics. The absence of spirituality in any of these areas represents a failure of faith. The expression of spiritual principles is often difficult and unrewarding; this is particularly so with regard to politics which is necessarily about conflicts of interest and opinion. It is however particularly important that spiritual principles operate in the political arena where decisions are made about matters affecting the whole of society over many years. It is the efforts of faith-inspired men and women which over the years has brought us the benefits of freedom, justice and democracy; these values are sometimes devalued by politicians who may find them inconvenient. It should be the responsibility of those with spiritual understanding and authority to hold politicians to account for the maintenance of essential standards, such as truthfulness, honesty, integrity.

In Britain we comfort ourselves with the belief that we enjoy a democratic political system. Such belief needs to be qualified by the well-known description of this system as an elective dictatorship. Once a party is elected to office it has almost absolute power. This situation can be, and has been, abused. Our supposedly democratic system is open to the corrupting effects of an unchecked executive, of patronage, spin, and economy with the truth. Humanity is susceptible to delusion, and none more so than politicians. When politicians have unchecked power, delusion and hubris can lead to disaster for everyone. This is especially true in today's interconnected world in which problems of horrifying dimensions are developing, as discussed later. It is no exaggeration to say that the very existence of society requires that humanity and its leaders face up to these problems in a righteous way – with courage, honesty and integrity.

Britain needs a spiritual authority with the ability to take a stand to defend essential values: righteousness, truthfulness, honesty, integrity, freedom, justice, democracy. Without such a spiritual authority, the level of political activity enters a downward spiral and ideologues create their own false gods that corrupt society. In other times people would look to the Church to provide a counter weight to the power of the State. In the present day, religious leaders in Britain seem powerless and have failed to defend essential values. Many politicians are happy for the Church to be neutered and to be unable to offer opposition to corruption.

Despite the present failures of Christian institutions it should be recognized that, throughout history, faith in God has inspired countless people in charitable and humanitarian endeavours; this applies even more in today's global village. The values of Christianity are woven deep into the fabric of our society; to try to remove them or to allow them to rot away would damage our society irretrievably. But these values are being eroded as a result of conflict between a mindless secular juggernaut and a weak church on unsound foundations. There are undoubtedly various cracks in the ramshackle edifice of Christianity built up by institutions over the centuries. The criticisms by atheists, justifiable in many ways, point to serious flaws in the way Christian doctrine has developed and is received in today's world. The Holy Bible itself was written and edited many years ago, by people who were motivated by their own particular interests in the limited world of which they had knowledge, to appeal to a very different population from that which exists now; since then scientific exploration of the nature of the earth and the universe has led to questioning of the factual veracity of the ancient scriptures. There is of course much wisdom in the scriptures; also there is much allegory because that is a very good way of conveying essential truths. Nevertheless it now seems ludicrous for any religion to claim that their God is the only God, that their teachings have divine authority. Surely, if there is a God – a Supreme Being – then there can be only one. However, it is not surprising that different peoples, different cultures have developed different ways of perceiving the same God, different ways of describing Him, different ways of worshiping Him, different ways of understanding the nature of God. Today's challenge, for those who recognize the value of religion, is to reform religious teachings to take account of the expansion of scientific knowledge and the nature of today's societies. Religion may then be able to play an effective part in encouraging leaders to follow a righteous path and avoid the temptation to create false gods.

The crises with which we are currently preoccupied and other looming crises suggest that the world is entering a period of great upheaval that requires a review of our belief systems; to decide on the essential principles that can guide us during these troubled times. It seems appropriate to consider ways in which our national religion – Christianity - might be strengthened using insights that are now available to us. I try in these essays to present a spiritual framework for what I believe is a God for the twenty first century and a basis for a religion that can provide an effective spiritual foundation for our nation.

Chapter 1

Evolution

If we are going to teach creation science as an alternative to evolution, then we should also teach the stork theory as an alternative to biological reproduction.

Judith Hayes

2009 is the bicentenary of the birth of Charles Darwin. In 1859 Darwin published "On the Origin of Species". An intellectual giant, Darwin proposed that all species of life have evolved over time from common ancestors through the process of natural selection. Although there had been earlier proposals for the idea of evolution this was the first description of the implacable evolutionary process through survival of the fittest, natural selection and continuation of species by reproduction.

The term 'natural selection' contrasts with 'artificial selection' in which human breeders of cows, horses or other animals deliberately bring about, over a period of time, desired changes in the characteristics of these animals by choosing mating partners. Thus horses are bred to run faster or to have greater stamina; cows are bred to provide more milk. 'Natural selection' takes place as part of the normal life process without any outside intervention.

The theory assumes that for any surviving species more creatures are brought into existence than are needed for the continuation of the species. For a variety of reasons some of these creatures do not survive long enough to mate. Only the fittest and best adapted to their environment survive to mate and reproduce. As part of this process there are random genetic mutations some of which are beneficial and are passed on to the next generation. Natural selection is the process by which favourable heritable traits become more common in successive generations and unfavourable heritable traits become less common.

The mechanism of natural selection enables evolution to take place within a population of organisms. Over a period of many generations there may be a gradual change in characteristics to adapt the species to its environment and improve its likelihood of survival. Over time beneficial mutations may accumulate to create an entirely different species.

Darwin's theories have been accepted by the scientific community and have provided the basis for much further scientific discovery. Natural selection has become one of the cornerstones of modern biology. In more recent times the theory of evolution has been complemented by the work of earth scientists who have estimated the age of the earth to be over 4 billion years as compared with the few thousand years of biblical estimates. It is particularly appropriate to consider the effect of evolution theory in 2009, not only because it is the bicentenary of Darwin's birth, but because of the relevance of this theory to the crises that presently threaten humanity.

It is instructive to consider Darwin himself in an evolutionary context. He was born in 1809 in the middle of the Industrial Revolution, a time of enormous change – technologically, economically, and socially. He published 'On the Origin of Species' in 1859 when the first oil well was being dug in the USA and where 2000 barrels of oil – the new elixir - were produced. The changes initiated by the Industrial Revolution were accelerated considerably by the availability of cheap oil as described in a later chapter. The advance in humanity's understanding of itself and its history provided by the theory of evolution matched the startling changes taking place in the material world; this new understanding had huge implications for religion.

Darwin conceived his theory in 1838 but was so concerned about the effect that it might have on the Christian consensus of the time that he waited over twenty years to publish it. Until 1859 the Christian consensus was built on a belief in the inerrant authority of the Holy Bible as the revealed word of God; priests operated as channels for the Holy Spirit; the ethical code that supported civilized life was drawn from the Bible's teachings. There can be nothing more absolute and convincing than edicts from a supreme God, so the structure of society rested on firm foundations. Ever since 1859 the Christian world has struggled to come to terms with Darwin's theory of evolution, and even now has not succeeded. Darwin replaced the certainty of Genesis, of Adam and Eve, and of the uniqueness of humans in a world created by God, with the apparent chaos of evolution. Ethical codes supported by the church no longer had divine authority. The Christian church struggled, trying to pretend nothing had happened, while the world moved on.

Since 1859 there have been immense material changes in the world. The oil consumption in the USA was a total of 2000 barrels in 1859, but by 2006 the world oil consumption had risen to 85 million barrels per day! World population has increased from less than 1 billion in 1859 to nearly 7 billion in 2009!

Unfortunately since 1859 Christian theology has stagnated, so that the vast material changes have lacked an appropriate ethical support.

The work of Darwin and subsequent biologists applies to the whole of earth's organisms but its significance for human life created religious controversy that still exists. Religionists have never quite come to terms with Darwin's theories which seemed to conflict with scriptural texts such as those describing the origins of humanity in the Garden of Eden; dislike even more the idea that man has descended from monkeys; and cannot countenance the scientific evidence that the earth is billions of years old. Religious opponents of Darwin's theories have developed their own theories, known as creationism, which adheres literally to biblical explanations of the origin of life.

The inability of religionists to adapt their religious doctrines to scientific evidence has weakened their religion and consequently its ability to play its part in the material world. The inertia of religious institutions has prevented them from embracing the theory of evolution, and recognizing that it is a remarkable explanation of a process overseen by God! The evolutionary process is not only a very elegant concept, but is also absolute and inexorable. It can be seen as a manifestation of God; not a God who defines every aspect of our existence but a God who supports our unfoldment. How else would a God have created the world we live in?

It is the sheer relentlessness of the evolutionary process which seems to contradict the concept of a loving God, and therefore disturbs some believers and gives comfort to atheists. It seems that religion, and society, has not come to terms with the idea that modern humans are the product of a millennia-long process of survival of the fittest, natural selection, random mutation and continuation of the species through procreation; nothing about love, compassion or equality here! Our very existence proves the virtue of pragmatism and survival. We, who are on earth today, have to recognize that we are the end result of this stark, relentless evolutionary process and that we have a part to play in the continuation of this process. Darwin's discovery has made it necessary to modify our understanding of the world's spiritual framework and of its central component – God.

We need to understand that while God is a loving God, the laws which He has created are implacable. This is the case with the biological evolutionary process where there has been little conscious individual human involvement. In human life the applicable law is that known as karma – as you sow so shall you reap – which is discussed in more detail later. This applies to both individuals and to groups of individuals, companies, and nations. The consequences of actions cannot ultimately be avoided, and it is the false belief that they can which leads to so much unhappiness.

Evolution of societies

The principle of evolution is majestic and ubiquitous, applying to every level of matter and organisms across the universe; it is a sublime expression of pragmatism. The humble motto "If it doesn't work fix it, if it works leave it alone" is a homely expression of evolution at a human level. The phrase "survival of the fittest" brutally describes the exciting evolutionary journey on which humanity and the whole of the universe is engaged. Darwin focused on biological evolution as applied to species, but the general principle of evolution has an application to all aspects of human life. Humans, at the peak of animal development, have invented sophisticated arrangements for organising the collective life of large groups of individuals; these institutions, societies, nations, civilizations are all subject to an evolutionary process which flows like a turbulent river. The characteristics that allow these groupings to prosper and survive are not the same as those required by individual humans. Humans require health, strength, stamina, agility, and intelligence to adapt to the environment and stand a better chance of survival. Societies require a set of rules that support collective life; without such a set of rules collective life disintegrates. These rules have generally been provided by religion. There have been many changes in the pattern of life throughout the world since 1859; unfortunately there has been no corresponding evolution in religious principles to provide an ethical basis for this new pattern of life.

Since 1859 there have been changes in political arrangements throughout the world; there have been huge developments in technology with consequential changes in the way humanity lives; there have been considerable changes in the pattern of international trade; there have been changes in the sophistication of international financial systems. Yet despite the immense impact of the theory of evolution on orthodox theology there seems to have been no adaptation of religious principles to support this new pattern of life.

All parts of human life are subject to the inexorable process of evolution that requires us to recognize that the continuation of our existence is not guaranteed; we have to arrange our lives in an appropriate way in order to survive. Evolution has brought humans to a peak of animal development, at which we can claim to be "made in the image of God" because we possess consciousness and free will and also extraordinary physical, mental and emotional abilities. Humans, particularly at the present stage of our global civilization, are able to influence the process of evolution in a way that was beyond the capabilities of earlier organisms. We are gods in the making and our time on earth might be considered as work experience or on-the-job training. Until homo sapiens appeared on the scene, the evolutionary process was overseen by God; now this responsibility is shared with humans. We have to ask ourselves if, individually and collectively, we are living in a way that facilitates the evolutionary journey on which humanity is engaged. This means exploring those matters which most deeply effect the quality of individual and collective life: sin, righteousness and a religion that fully encompasses the theory of evolution.

The significance of evolution for a nation such as Britain is that its existence in any particular form is not guaranteed. Past civilizations such as Greece, Egypt and Rome have faded away under the remorseless process of evolution. We in Britain have a choice; we can adopt deliberately policies that will enable our nation - with its values, its culture, its religion - to survive, or we can simply drift down a path determined by passing fancies that must end inevitably in sadness, disappointments, regret, recriminations.

The first prerequisite for Britain to survive is a code of ethics which clearly defines the difference between righteousness and sin; and which generally advocates and supports high standards of behaviour throughout society. A society without high standards of behaviour degenerates in all spheres of activity whether personal relationships, business activities, or governance.

In an evolutionary world of constant change, who should we expect to offer guidance on survival? The time span of politicians, and their selfish interests, are too limited. Paradoxically religion, that was seemingly cast into oblivion by the theory of evolution, is the only institution with a time span, a depth of interest and a level of integrity that enable it to advise on how to live in an evolving world. Religion, with its concern for man's immortal soul, should be seen as a source of guidance in this world of constant flux. Religion is not a thing apart, only concerned with its limited parochial environment, but can offer spiritual advice in the wider temporal world.

Those with faith can seek God's guidance in facing the challenges of the modern world. However they need a religion that fully encompasses the theory of evolution and is appropriate for the twenty-first century.

Chapter 2

Sin and Society

Fools make a mock at sin.
                    Holy Bible, Proverbs 14.9

Is sin an out-of-date concept in the 3rd millennium? Is there much point in discussing it except as a historic curiosity? Is the concept so repugnant to modern man and woman that it is hardly worth examining? Is there still a need for moral guidance, and what form might it take? These are some of the questions posed by the word that has become unmentionable.

Sin was once considered to be a transgression against divine law, but after Darwin questioned the infallibility of the Bible and Nietzsche proclaimed that "God is dead", the aversion to sin diminished, with considerable effect on human behaviour. What then is the relationship between sin and the divine?

A cynical explanation of the discovery of the divine is that way back in prehistory, the leader of a tribe realised that one way to explain things he didn't understand to his followers, and thus retain credibility, was to attribute such mysteries to supernatural powers or gods. The concept became more useful as the leader became older, and less able to maintain power through physical strength, agility and quick reactions; he could claim to be an intermediary with the gods, to have acquired some of their magical powers, and could use this reflected glory to control the tribe. Divinity was thereby invented and the leader became a shaman or witch doctor.

In prehistory there were many mysteries: Where does rain come from? Why does it fall on some days and not on others? What is thunder? What is lightning? The awe in which the gods were held was proportional to the number of unexplained mysteries. The shaman quickly realised that this awe of the divine gave him power to command his tribe; he was able to proclaim observances and abstentions on the basis that he was so instructed by the gods. This was the beginning of a moral code and sin. Sin was not simply wrongdoing; as a transgression against everything that was held most awesome it was invested with immense feelings of guilt, shame and fear of divine punishment.

Over time the concepts were refined and applied around the world, from the Pharaohs of Egypt, to the Incas of Peru, to the Spanish Inquisition. Religion took out a copyright on sin. Leaders used the power of divinity in a variety of ways, from the well meaning to the self-serving. Religion tended to condemn anything it didn't like as sinful which resulted in sin and morality being inextricably associated with religion, so that rebellion against one implied rebellion against both.

An unfortunate consequence of the belief in divine authority and its expectation of unquestioning obedience, has been the adoption of God as a role model by political leaders throughout history. Many rulers have found it expedient to control their subjects through a claim to divine inspiration, like Charles I, or a similar claim to inspiration by substitute divinity, like Stalin and Hitler. Such regimes, that robbed the population of the ability to develop their own moral code and standards of behaviour, invariably came to an abrupt end, since they lacked the self-regulating effect of democracy.

Gradually, as mystery after mystery has been explained by science, as the life of modern man has become ever more independent of unexplained phenomena, the awe in which the divine is held has diminished, the power of religion has crumbled and the concept of sin has withered. This withering has been accompanied, not surprisingly, by a process of social disintegration. This seems an appropriate time to review the concept of sin, avoiding preconceptions about its divine ordinance, but bearing in mind that warnings about sin may seem arid unless presented as part of a complete philosophy that includes an uplifting principle and the possibility of repentance, redemption and forgiveness. Religion has coupled gloomy warnings about sin with the inspirational qualities of divinity:

"Hear again my Word supreme, the deepest secret of silence. Because I love thee well, I will speak to thee words of salvation. Give thy mind to me, and give me thy heart, and thy sacrifice, and thy adoration. This is my Word of promise: thou shalt in truth come to me, for thou art dear to me. Leave all things behind, and come to me for thy salvation. I will make thee free from the bondage of sins. Fear no more"
(Krishna speaking in Bhagavad Gita, 18.64-66)

Teachings about sin are likely to be effective only if they are associated with an uplifting principle which identifies a supreme goal that supports and justifies the avoidance of sin, through hope for the future. Such an uplifting principle does not have to be divinity, but simply the highest principle that the individual chooses e.g. humanity, the planet, or nature.

As part of the popular rejection of the religious connotations of sin, there has been a retreat from the idea of original sin, the belief that mankind has an innate liability to sin, or to put it another way, is far from perfect and has a tendency to make mistakes that may range from the thoughtlessly trivial to the deliberately devastating. The comforting philosophy that humans are fundamentally good has been widely adopted, accompanied by an aversion to the responsibility of judgement. Rather than focusing on behaviour that is dysfunctional (sin) and looking at ways to discourage it, we divert our energies to a search for possible justifications of such behaviour, as if the concept of sin has become so intolerable that we have to prove that everyone is good.

Discrimination and judgement are part of everyday life yet the terms have acquired a curious notoriety. Public discussions of sensitive matters have become very delicate, with a neurotic avoidance of anything resembling criticism or blame. Nevertheless, positive aspects of discrimination, judgement and blame are certainly involved in concepts of sin and sinfulness.

A good illustration of the nature of sin is the list of seven deadly sins that is just as relevant today as when it was first formulated in the 6th century: pride, greed, lust, anger, gluttony, envy, and sloth. These are not actions or behaviour, but rather deep unconscious motivations that take root in the psyche like a parasite and so eat into the essential integrity of its host, that the individual loses the sense of identity and, ultimately, contact with reality. Unable to moderate this compulsive motivation by rational processes, the individual loses command of their own will. The difficulty of dealing with these deeply unconscious and often addictive motivations, is increased by denial of the condition, and of the problems it brings.

Such sins are deep-seated corrosive attitudes that rob an individual of their conscious will, prevent them playing a normal part in society and form a breeding ground for dysfunctional behaviour that is damaging to self and to others. Moral sickness is often a cocktail of sins; pride, sloth and denial of reality are a potent mixture, when bigotry (pride) supported by a lack of analysis (sloth) results in a denial of reality. Sins may range from the attitudes already mentioned, to the sinful thoughts, behaviour and actions that are produced by such attitudes. However it is arguable that the worst sin, the culmination of others, is denial of reality, since it removes all hope for the individual to engage positively with the real world. Instead they try to impose their own petty dogma on the world's majestic reality. A society composed of such individuals is a recipe for conflict and sounds like a dialogue from a pantomime: "Oh yes it is." "Oh no it isn't..."

Sin is not an abstract concept, gratuitously invented by religion to make life difficult for sinners. Sin is very real and warnings against it are part of guidance for a fulfilled life in a world beset by temptation. They represent wisdom accumulated since the beginning of time that was endorsed by religion and given the added force of divine authority. The experience of many generations is that the attractive force of sin is very powerful, that it is very easy to succumb to its temptations, and that it is only prior knowledge about sin that gives us a chance of resisting it. The guidance has evolved to help mankind resist the temptation of sinning and so avoid damage to themselves and others. The avoidance of sin is not easy, and it is part of the function of society and its various institutions, to create a structure that enables members of society to avoid sin, rather than encouraging them to be sinful. A value of the teachings about sin is that they cater for everyone and particularly for the large majority of ordinary people who are hit hardest by the suffering that results from sin.

The concept of sin is relevant to both individual and collective life, because it provides guidance and structure. It is a critical part of the interaction between the individual and the collective, because the definition of sin has to be formulated collectively, but applies to the individual. It relates to interactions between individuals and also between the individual and the collective. It represents one of the tools that mankind has available to enable individuals to live and work together, and to determine the evolutionary direction of society.

The emotional force of divine condemnation of sin was used effectively to counter balance the power of the seven deadly sins. Without the control of this emotional force, sin flourishes, and the seven deadly sins are much in evidence in Britain today. Expedience rules with a maxim that operates at the highest levels of society: "If is not illegal, then do it; if it is illegal, do it but don't get caught." Sins motivate not only individuals but also large groups, and may even be cultivated and exploited. Individual sins, reinforced by collective expression, are enormously powerful; it is demonstrable (e.g. in Nazi Germany) how irrational attitudes can be so reinforced in groups as to become wild obsession. When we look at present-day Britain, we see that it is not only individuals that have their wills hijacked by unconscious forces but our collective institutions; we see a correlation between national problems and sin.

The first aspect of Britain to examine is the condition of our society, because this affects every citizen intimately and influences all other aspects; it is also a case history of the corrosive influence of different types of sin. There is no lack of apologists for the condition of society, which it is said is a natural development that we all have to live with. The apologists generally come from the group of clever, astute, ruthless, beautiful or wealthy people who can manage well in any situation, including anarchy; additionally they may actually benefit in various ways from the deterioration in society. Unfortunately it is generally the innocent, the naive, the trusting, and the tenderhearted who suffer from such deterioration.

Apologists may dismiss criticism of today's society as "moral panic", but proof of the subversion of society's basic structure comes from the most authoritative quarters: "...there needs to be public awareness of the social disaster that lies ahead if family life continues to fragment at the present rate. The combined statistics and research data present an alarming picture of social disintegration and violence if present trends continue." This frightening warning was not given by a puritanical preacher, but by the sober members of the Lords and Commons Family and Child Protection Group in their report to the Home Secretary in 1998, over ten years ago. This is only one of a plethora of grave warnings given by a variety of social commentators, but it is sufficiently authoritative and serious to warrant deep public concern.

The social disintegration to which they refer - social deprivation, poverty, child abuse, low educational attainment, unemployment, alcoholism, drug abuse, civic deterioration, and crime - is a consequence of the erosion of marriage that has always been a basic element in stable and advanced societies. This erosion of marriage has taken place against the wishes of the large majority of the population, under successive governments, over a period of four decades. There is no shortage of statistics to confirm what is happening; one of the most significant is that over 40% of children are now born outside marriage, many of them to single mothers. Four decades ago there was general understanding that single motherhood was detrimental for all concerned: deprivation for mother and child, exclusion of fathers from the satisfaction and responsibilities of fatherhood, and instability for society. Yet Government, heedless of the warnings given by many authorities, denies the significance of marriage and insists that the conditions of never-married motherhood, teenage motherhood, underage motherhood, cohabiting parenthood, parenthood with two same sex "parents", single parenthood, and parenthood with two married heterosexual parents are all equally valid! Government denies the need for an institutional framework to guide individual behaviour, has removed any differential support for marriage, but pretends to be surprised at the resultant social disintegration. This seems to be evidence of the worst sin – denial of reality.

If we examine the contributors to the process of social disintegration we see that significant elements are consumerism and sex. Consumerism has brought many advantages but relies on, exploits and encourages most of the seven deadly sins, directly or indirectly. The power of the cocktail of consumerism and sex, laced with the seven deadly sins, has proved irresistible. The process began some 50 years ago when the process of sexual liberation blew away inhibitions and released the genie of sex from its bottle. It had been put there by those who were aware of the power of sex, of the temptation of lust, and the possibly disastrous consequences of succumbing to it; they attempted to maintain marriage as a positive way of harnessing the power of sex for the benefit of all. There were others who objected to such repression; the genie promised exciting sexual pleasure unconstrained by possibilities of conception, or the practical difficulties of relationship and parenthood, so the cork was pulled. The very idea of sexual freedom focuses solely on the physical enjoyment of sex, and warnings that sex involved more than physical pleasure were ignored.

We now have to live with the effects of a genie on the loose - a swirling, exciting, capricious and tumultuous energy that operates in an uncontrolled way, often with destructive effects on individual lives and society. And the genie is simply energy, it doesn't have a mind or a conscience, so cannot really be blamed for the mayhem it creates. The responsibility for guiding and directing sexual energy can only be assumed by human consciousness, individual and collective. Energy, if it is employed with an appreciation of its capabilities and dangers, can be used effectively for the benefit of all. Energy that is allowed to operate with no kind of direction, becomes an arbitrary, uncontrollable monster; the greater the energy, the greater the monster, and sex is one of the greatest energies we know. This is why the wise have always warned about the sins associated with sex.

Yet sex as a public policy issue is not being addressed with any direction or cohesion; it has been left as a no-man's land into which self-motivated groups launch themselves to gain some advantage, and in which particular issues are fought over and sometimes settled on a piecemeal basis. We threw away the rule book for the sexual game when we set the genie free, and in a game without rules, without structure, the winner is the player who is the most ruthless, the worst bully, the meanest manipulator, and who has the least conscience - in short the most sinful. The losers are the trusting, the innocent, the naive, the gullible, and the vulnerable. This is a world in which the barricades to damaging behaviour, provided by the concept of sin, have been removed.

The media's embrace of the genie provides a frenzied display of Dionysian abandonment. Sex is a powerful vehicle for those who, for whatever reason, wish to excite, shock or draw attention to themselves. Newspapers, magazines, books, television, entertainers use sex to excite and thereby increase sales and profit. Advertisements use sex as a primary tool to attract and persuade potential customers. Other commercial interests - alcohol, tobacco - enjoy the rewards that a partnership with the genie can bring. Special interest groups join in the free-for-all to obtain some particular advantage. The result of all this is that the public, particularly the young and vulnerable, are subjected to an unbalanced representation of sex that exploits a very natural interest and curiosity, that excites without satisfying, and that completely ignores the wider dimensions. The media scene, without effective regulation, presents a collage of all the seven deadly sins.

There are other challenging social issues but the critical aspect of sex that makes it a central issue is its involvement with the whole business of reproduction: conception, pregnancy, birth and the raising of children, our future citizens. These children carry with them into the future, the attitudes and behavioural patterns that they acquire in their formative years. Any negative influences on children are propagated into, and determine the characteristics of, future society. Such negative influences are all too easy to identify.

The present condition of society is commonly attributed to the free choice of the public, but in fact the public has had far less influence on the developing condition of society than it had when the standards of morality were strongly influenced by the church. The public, passive subjects of a consumer society, have been conditioned by various special interest groups motivated by combinations of the seven deadly sins. The engine of consumerism, fuelled by sex, has powered social developments while those with some responsibility for the moral state of society have simply stood aside. Authority in the form of government, the law, and to a lesser extent the church refuses to support the institution of marriage because, they say, it would be discriminatory.

The greatest sin exhibited in the developing saga of our social condition is the denial of reality, and it is this sin that is so apparent in much of the rest of public affairs. It is paradoxical that our country has been a democracy for longer than most other countries, that our standard of life is immensely better than in many other countries, that we have been at peace for over sixty years, that we enjoy the advantages of incredibly advanced technology, that Government has a huge budget and is sufficiently powerful to be described as an "elective dictatorship"; yet Britain is so plagued by a catalogue of chronic problems that we seem to have lost our collective mind. Our collective mind is not behaving rationally but, in the grip of parasitical unconscious motivations, is unable to engage with reality; in other words it has drifted into the worst sin.

George Orwell in his book *Nineteen Eighty-Four* described 'Doublethink' as 'the power of holding two contradictory beliefs in one's mind simultaneously, and accepting both of them'. Doublethink, invented for the brutal totalitarian world of *Nineteen Eighty-Four*, seemed a recipe for madness but is apparent in the drift away from reality in public affairs.

Democracy is concerned with collective life, with the relationship between those who govern and the governed, and with the way in which decisions are made on behalf of the collective. Britain undoubtedly has a collective existence; the fact that the State collects nearly half our income as taxes and spends it on our behalf emphasises our existence as a collective entity over and above that of our individual lives. But does Britain have a collective mind? The structure for a mind is evident. We have a Government that is in charge of spending all those billions of pounds; we have Houses of Parliament where hundreds of Members of Parliament and of Lords can interrogate the Government on their conduct of the nation's affairs; we have Select Committees who can question the highest and the lowest in the land to discover the truth; we have a media with thousands of journalists investigating issues and making public their conclusions; we have an established Church (and many unestablished churches) to give spiritual guidance; we have think tanks that look into the future and make predictions for the areas of life that they believe are critical for our collective existence. Yet we seem to be plagued by man-made disasters. Why is it that some things go so disastrously wrong over such a long period of time, giving the impression that our collective mind is just a black hole?

It seems ridiculous to have all the trappings of a mind, yet to have mislaid its functions, including will. Our collective will, together with its supporting structures, appears to have withered. That robust symbol of Britain, John Bull, seems to have metamorphosed into a Frankenstein monster with a lobotomy, a low attention span, and a short memory - feeble rather than frightening. The pathetic creature staggers along, confused by contradictory thoughts, driven by instinct and unaware of the debris of policy disasters that litters his path. Like a child with a music box, the monster responds with some enthusiasm to the prospect of Olympic Games, but on deeper multi-faceted issues exhibits little awareness, no ability to make connections, no ability to analyse or discriminate, no ability to make conscious choices and pursue them with determination. John Bull seems to lack a sense of identity; he doesn't know who he is, where he is going, what he wants to achieve. These are the wages of sin.

In addition to the social disintegration that has been discussed, that is itself catastrophic, some chronic disasters that afflict John Bull and demonstrate the confusion that grips him are: the transport problem, the crisis in the countryside and agriculture, unbalanced regional development, membership of the European Union, crime.

JB wants cars, wants the jobs involved in making cars, and wants the vast amounts of money gained from taxing road transport, but doesn't like spending money on roads and transport infrastructure. JB wants railways but doesn't like spending money on them either.

JB likes the idea of an idyllic countryside, but cannot arrange that farmers receive a sufficient return to stay in business, or that the rural infrastructure is adequate to support rural communities.

JB complains about economic overheating in the south, with excessive house building on green field sites. He complains about unemployment, dereliction, and communal decay in the north. At the same time he supports policies that make regional development more unbalanced.

JB likes to be involved with the European Union. While he doesn't want to give up sovereignty to a centralised federal state, he refuses to admit that a centralised federal state is the precise goal of most of the other members.

JB doesn't like crime, but in the face of the increasing crime that results from the social disintegration already mentioned, he finds it difficult to discriminate between criminals and victims. He reduces the effectiveness of the police force through bureaucracy and political correctness.

JB doesn't like alcohol-fuelled rowdiness and violence but worsens the problem by extending opening hours of licensed premises.

JB gets involved in wars but doesn't want to provide adequate funds for the Armed Forces.

The result of this indecision is confusion, chaos and suffering. We, the citizens of Britain, seem to be in the grip of the Titanic syndrome of avoidance, otherwise called the sin of denial of reality: the ship is unsinkable, the captain is such a nice man, the band plays beautifully, and we don't want to alarm the passengers. There seems to be collusion between all the main participants to avoid addressing the real problems, which might damage vested interests and deeply rooted prejudices. The government of the day and its supporting establishment, maintains the fiction that everything is under control, that whatever needs to be done is being done. The power of patronage is so great that most institutions follow the lead of the Government. We, the public, are preoccupied with our personal life and painfully aware of our inability to influence collective decisions. We desensitise ourselves to the pain of life by an appropriate anaesthetic, and in a state of complacency and wishful thinking, we are happy to be reassured that everything is fine.

This picture of contemporary Britain demonstrates the effects of sin in both individual and collective life. Society, having lost the protection given by a code of morality, is disintegrating under the effect of various forces including the alliance between consumerism and sex, with the only compensation being an uneven rise in material standards of life. We should not expect humans to be perfect, and that events will always be in our favour. Adversity, misunderstanding, delusion, wishful thinking, and complacency commonly occur and have to be endured. However the present situation does not resonate with the authenticity expected in the third millennium and is unsustainable; if historic teachings about sin are unacceptable, we need to find an alternative.

Are rules for behaviour appropriate in a society that already has so many laws, regulations and directives but is awash in moral relativism? Life in present society demonstrates that laws cannot force people to behave in ways that are beneficial for themselves and for the general community; despite this our society layers one ineffective law on another, when what it actually needs are generally accepted standards of personal conduct. There is, indeed, a need for a set of guidelines for life in the third millennium, for a global world whose citizens become ever more interdependent.

Such a set of guidelines would not replace the secular laws that proliferate throughout society, but would offer guidance that helps individuals to deal with the challenges that confront them, to help them live effectively with others in the world, and to help them evolve. To serve the needs of the modern world, the guidelines need to serve both those who acknowledge some form of divinity and those who do not, without making judgements. Those who acknowledge divinity are already open to the teachings of a moral code. A challenge for new guidelines is to convince those who don't acknowledge divinity of the need and value of such a code. The greatest challenge, however, is to persuade those in authority to support a moral code, since it becomes worthless if it is undermined by those – in politics, the law, education, public administration and the media – who have a duty to support and maintain a social structure that discourages sin.

If the bad news for believers of religious teachings about sin is that some people reject religion, the good news is that sin can be disconnected from religion. The value of a moral code is not affected by the source of its inspiration. We don't need divine authority to prove that some behaviours are beneficial and some are detrimental. It is observable and demonstrable that some life styles are conducive to lasting happiness, while other lifestyles that may be pleasurable in the short term, bring only suffering in the long term. This applies both to the individual and the collective, in that particular behaviour may bring suffering, not only to the individual, but to society in general; the corollary is that society has a proper interest not only in determining its own characteristics, but in ensuring that the behaviour of individuals does not endanger the existence of society.

It is not surprising that religious teachings often make much practical sense; divine exhortations would not be acceptable on a lasting basis if they were not practical in the world we live in. The Christian religion has existed for two thousand years because its teachings meet the pragmatic needs of life on earth, and have enabled a highly civilised society to evolve. Of course, some people find that the significance of a moral code is enhanced by the endorsement of divine authority; however such endorsement is not essential. "Morality" does not have to be ordained by God but is simply a word to describe behaviour that brings lasting happiness.

All that we need to guide us in life is with us here and now. As Indian Tantric philosophy says, "What is here, is elsewhere. What is not here, is nowhere." A valuable guide to life is the teaching of the Dalai Lama that the purpose of life is the pursuit of happiness. His happiness is not the hedonistic variety but one that transcends time and space; it is a lasting happiness that recognises the interconnectedness of all life. It is actually to our advantage to pursue lasting happiness for ourselves and for those around us. A moral code based on the pursuit of lasting happiness must inevitably include a warning against sin, whatever words might be used to suit a politically correct climate. We can no longer try to deal with sin by pretending it doesn't exist. A moral code offers a means for modern society to extricate itself from the disintegration that threatens to engulf it.

Chapter 3

Righteousness and Religion

Righteousness exalteth a nation.
Holy Bible, Proverbs 14.34

Righteousness has become unfashionable in recent times; it is annoying for people who are preoccupied with the immediate gratification of material desires to have to consider a "right" course of action. However as a result of the current global financial problems, commentators are beginning to talk about "doing what is right" as an alternative to doing what is immediately attractive.

Righteousness needs to be examined in depth because it is a quality that directly facilitates human evolution but which is sadly lacking in today's society. The need for a concept of "righteousness" arises from the existence of humans at the peak of the evolutionary chain; with consciousness, free will and such extraordinary physical, mental and emotional abilities that they can claim to have been created "in the image of God"! Unfortunately they do not possess the wisdom of God, but instead are predisposed to what some Christians call "original sin". Humans are like children set loose in a firework factory, completely unaware of the damage they can do to themselves and others. They need guidance on how to live, how to think; although with supreme arrogance they may resist proffered advice. "Righteousness" is the name of the standard of behaviour that has, over millennia, been developed to encourage humans to behave and think in a constructive and sustainable way. The first sentence of *Anna Karenina* by Leo Tolstoy reads: "Happy families are all alike; every unhappy family is unhappy in its own way". Similarly, in any given situation there is one way to be righteous but a great many ways to be unrighteous.

In addressing "righteousness" it is not my intention to tell individuals how to behave; they have the free will to decide for themselves. However I try to raise awareness that actions have consequences and that unrighteous behaviour may have unpleasant consequences for the individual concerned and for wider society. Additionally leaders of society may make momentous decisions with huge consequences for everyone. These leaders are given control of a large proportion of society's resources and can call on the advice of a large body of public servants; it is reasonable for society to demand that these leaders act in a righteous way. It is unrighteous for leaders to choose a path that leads to an evolutionary dead end and has unpleasant consequences for many people.

Psychology teaches that humans have a lower unconscious and a higher unconscious. The lower unconscious is the location of material impulses – need for food, drink, entertainment, excitement, sex – and the destructive emotions that result from having these needs frustrated – anger, envy, jealousy, resentment, rage, contempt, hatred. The higher unconscious is the location of conscience, love, compassion, charity, spiritual intelligence, spiritual intuition and respect for truth. It is through the higher unconscious that we can perceive the right way to live despite the distractions with which the world surrounds us. These distractions are reinforced by delusion – the delusion that the source of happiness lies in the satisfaction of the material desires that originate in the lower unconscious.

The nature of human life is that we are confronted by challenges that require choices: we can choose right action, but delusion always confuses us with a seductive promise of an easier way, a more profitable way, a quicker way to greater happiness. History shows that delusion does not discriminate between people; the exalted and the highly intelligent are just as susceptible as the most humble. Humans are constantly exposed to temptations that appeal to greed for food, to greed for wealth, to the desire for power, to sexual desire; with the promise that all these things can be obtained without any penalties. That is the delusion; but all these things have a price which we only discover when it is too late to avoid paying it. Ultimately there is only one way that humans can find true and lasting happiness; that is through right action or righteousness.

Civilisations require an ethical code as a basis for life in society, and generally they find that code from a religion. "Righteousness" is the quality that is needed to abide by a code of ethics. The path of spiritual development and effective, harmonious life in the community both depend on the quality of righteousness. Without righteousness, there is a downward spiritual spiral and communal life becomes more combative, nihilistic and squalid. For most of us, our behaviour regrettably falls short on the scale of righteousness, but we can still value it and aspire to it.

Righteousness is a reflection of God – however God is understood - in human life. God is the highest principle we can conceive, being described by religions in terms such as: Exalted, Almighty, Lord, King, Everlasting. Righteousness, or right action, is so significant for human life that it is appropriate for it to be associated with and supported by this highest principle.

Righteousness is a way of life that is embraced by most religions both as a path to God and as an eminently practical way to live and find happiness in the world. Despite the belief by some that righteousness is puritanical, painful and repressive, one would not expect a God to approve ways of living that were impractical or destructive or unnecessarily difficult to abide by. Righteousness - a central belief in most religions - implies a range of human qualities and behaviours that are necessary in any society to enable people to live together in a peaceful and vibrant way, whereas unrighteousness is bad both for the individual and for society, leading to conflict, corruption, decadence and anarchy. It is therefore not surprising that most religions propose similar guidelines. Righteousness is not something to be feared, or dismissed as only an attribute of archbishops. Those who choose to follow the path of righteousness can be sure of God's love and help.

One of the many factors influencing the presence of righteousness in society is vocabulary:

"When society was more religious and its vocabulary portrayed a God, people actually behaved in a way that accorded with the existence of a God. The mere act of describing a God actually affected people and their behaviour and had a real effect on the way that the world was. It is not that we have less evidence of a God now, simply that the idea of a God has been dropped by the vocabulary of society and that has actually changed people's behaviour and hence, the world."

(Laura Moralee, Independence, October 2008)

Words have power; this power is understood and used by advertisers and politicians to influence the way people perceive the world, the way they think and act. In the field of religion there is a close relationship between the words that are used and people's perception and behaviour. When society was more religious a spiritual vocabulary was used that included words such as divinity, sacredness, righteousness and sin. "Divinity" and "sacredness" represented the highest spiritual principle, "righteousness" represented a way of life on earth that accorded with an ethical code and "sin" represented a significant deviation from this ethical code. The vocabulary conveyed a sense of the significant difference between these qualities.

A society that aspires to be righteous needs a vocabulary that has the capability of describing and discriminating between the sacred and the profane – the highest and the lowest. Our present day usage of words has been corrupted so that words such as "sinful", "wicked", "evil" which once had very negative connotations are now used flippantly to convey the idea of "naughty but nice"; this is the "flat world" referred to by Ronald Reagan, a world without the ability to discriminate between different levels of human behaviour. Society needs a vocabulary that has the ability to discriminate between different levels of sacredness and profanity, and not to be afraid to use these levels.

God is normally the yard stick by which we define sacredness. God's qualities are omniscience, omnipotence, transcendence, immanence, absoluteness, purity, truthfulness – there is nothing higher or greater than God. Anything sacred is invested with the holy qualities of God. Thus churches and hymns have a sacred quality because they are dedicated to God and are infused with devotion. Human life is seen as sacred. An aspect of human life that has, throughout history, been considered as sacred is the duality of masculine and feminine, the process of sexual attraction, sexual union, procreation and the raising of children. Different societies and religions throughout the world have invested this area of life with the attributes of sacredness because it was concerned with something miraculous – the creation of new life, and thus the continued existence of the family, the tribe, the nation and the species. A major Christian festival is Christmas which in celebrating the birth of Jesus effectively celebrates and honours the birth of new human life regardless of status and thereby dignifies the mother and father of such new life.

Those who find it difficult to accept the idea of God will, unless they are very cynical, revere some other higher principle – maybe humanity itself, or the earth planet, or the universe. They can consider righteousness as a secular quality, similar to the concept of sustainability which is now well understood. Based on the belief that survival is a virtue, sustainability is now generally accepted as a desirable quality. Righteousness is simply the concept of sustainability applied to the human mind and human behaviour. Behaviour that is unrighteous is damaging, to the individual and/or society, leads down an evolutionary blind alley and in the long term is unsustainable.

Religions do not, of course, offer a legalistic form of guidelines – a sort of Napoleonic code that precisely defines what one should and should not do in a civilized society - since it is impossible to foresee the entire range of practices human ingenuity will discover and indulge in. For example, one would not expect the Christian Bible to condemn the use of a mobile phone while driving, however unrighteous we may believe it to be today. However a reading of ancient scriptures provides an understanding of righteousness that is acceptable to most people who are concerned for a civilized foundation for society.

The Ten Commandments which according to Biblical texts were delivered by God on Mount Sinai, obviously reflects the Middle Eastern society for whom they were written and have to be interpreted with that in mind; nevertheless they contain much wisdom:

- I am the Lord your God and you shall have no other gods before me.
- You shall not make yourself an idol.
- You shall not make wrongful use of the name of God.
- Remember the Sabbath and keep it holy.
- Honour your father and mother.
- You shall not kill.
- You shall not commit adultery.
- You shall not steal.
- You shall not bear false witness against your neighbour.
- You shall not covet your neighbour's wife or anything that belongs to your neighbour.

Jesus offered two commandments:

You shall love the Lord your God with all your heart, with all your soul and with all your mind. This is the greatest and first commandment.

And a second is like it: You shall love your neighbour as yourself. On these two commandments hang all the law and the prophets.

To complement these commandments Christianity has identified seven deadly sins:

Lust – Gluttony – Greed – Sloth – Wrath – Envy – Pride.

Some 2000 years ago an Indian sage distilled the accumulated wisdom concerning the principles of yoga philosophy and presented them in "The Yoga Sutras of Patanjali", which is in effect an ethical code underlying the quality of righteousness. The roots of the word "yoga" have a similar meaning to the roots of the word "religion": to bind. The wisdom contained in this book is timeless and applies to all humanity. Two sutras in particular are relevant, concerning *yama*, or abstention, and *niyama*, or observance; I give below my understanding of these:

YAMAS or abstentions

- Abstain from harming others; nonviolence (ahimsa).
- Abstain from falsehood; be truthful and honest (satya).
- Abstain from theft; do not steal (asteya).
- Abstain from incontinence; avoid meaningless sexual encounters and activities (brahmacharya).
- Abstain from greed; non-possessiveness (aparigraha).

NIYAMAS or observances

- Purity (shauca); keep your body, mind, emotions, clothing, surroundings clean. Eat healthy food.
- Contentment (santosha); cultivate contentment and tranquility.
- Austerity (tapas); show discipline in body, mind and speech.
- Study of the sacred text (svadhyaya); education uplifts, and study of texts that you find sacred will inspire you.
- Devotion to God (ishvara-pranidhana); live with an awareness of the divine.

Similar guidance for sustainable life is given by the Buddhist Noble Eightfold Path:

Wisdom
- Right View (includes moral law of karma)
- Right Intention

Ethical Conduct

- Right Speech
- Right Action
- Right Likelihood

Mental Discipline

- Right Effort
- Right Mindfulness
- Right Concentration

The creation of the Ten Commandments and similar moral codes are evidence of man's realization of the need for moral guidance. In the light of the theory of evolution it can be seen that humans are, indeed, God-like in the sense of their enhanced mental and physical abilities, but not God-like in terms of their discrimination and judgement; they therefore need guidance to encourage the expression of their abilities in positive ways rather than the extraordinary number of negative ways that are available to them. It follows from the code of ethics that some behaviour can be described as virtuous or righteous while some behaviour is at least questionable and even sinful; some behaviour should be welcomed and some behaviour is undesirable. As humans, major players in life's wonderful adventure, we need to play our part by discriminating between different behaviours, by making judgements on these behaviours. If we fail to do this we corrupt the process of human evolution.

It was natural for the leaders of early societies to depict a God as anthropomorphic and to claim that this God had defined a set of ethical codes, to invest them with greater authority. In our present society it is appropriate to recognize that ethical codes are not defined by God, but are set and nurtured by man; the corollary is that in our present society ethical codes are unrespected and even abused by those in authority.

Chapter 4

Reincarnation

*I give you the end of a golden string,
Only wind it into a ball,
It will lead you in at Heaven's Gate
Built in Jerusalem's Wall.*

William Blake

Man is a soul and he has a body. This short sentence represents the essence of the theory of reincarnation. Man is an immortal soul and for a relatively short period of time is incarnated into a physical body with which he becomes so identified that he loses his sense of immortality and becomes besotted with the senses, the instincts, the motivations and the fears of his temporary residence. This loss of a sense of immortality is apparent in most human activities, including those having a religious element. It is difficult to separate oneself from obsession with the physical body when one believes that it is all one has, apart from a nebulous possibility of a post-demise elevation to heaven.

The doctrine of reincarnation is a central tenet of many religious beliefs and was once embraced by early Christians. The belief that man is made in the image of God is a reflection of the fact that he is a soul with accompanying qualities of consciousness and free will, and has a body at the peak of the evolutionary chain with remarkable physical and mental abilities.

According to the doctrine of reincarnation, when someone dies their soul lives on and at some future time may be reborn into another body. The purpose of life is spiritual evolution to the point of achieving liberation from the necessity of being reborn, and becoming one with God. Until this point is reached the soul is constrained to be continually reborn into an earthly body. Each lifetime presents challenges and opportunities to evolve further. The individual has free will in responding to these challenges; he may evolve further or regress, and he may or may not choose to seek God's ever-present help.

The doctrine of reincarnation is complemented by the concept of karma which refers to the effects of past actions from the present or previous lifetimes. The self-regulating law of karma, as expounded in the Hindu scriptures, is that of action and reaction, cause and effect, sowing and reaping. Every human being by his thoughts and actions shapes his own destiny. Whatever energies he himself, wisely or unwisely has set in motion must return to him as their starting point, like a circle inexorably completing itself. An understanding of karma as the law of justice serves to free the human from resentment against God and man. A person's karma follows him from incarnation to incarnation until fulfilled or spiritually transcended.

The cumulative actions of human beings within communities, nations or the world as a whole constitute mass karma, which produces local or far-ranging effects according to the degree and preponderance of good or evil. The thoughts and actions of every human being, therefore, contribute to the good or ill of this world and all peoples in it.

The concept of mass karma is particularly important in today's world when the state has become so powerful in many countries. An all-powerful state can, on its own initiative, take momentous decisions. Governments can, like individuals, fall victims to temptation. They can, to court popularity, lead the people to believe that there is an easy path to happiness, when in fact this "easy" path only accumulates bad karma and leads to sorrow and suffering. When governments suffer from delusion, and lose sight of the need for righteousness, it is the ordinary people who accumulate bad karma and have to live with the consequences. There is a need for those with spiritual authority for the protection of righteousness to be willing to challenge delusion on the part of government, and to contribute to a truly democratic system of government.

References to "good" karma and "bad" karma illustrate the way past actions influence the life of a human being. "Bad" karma recalls the tale of the Ancient Mariner who had to live with the consequences of killing an albatross. However I reject the simplistic notion that anyone suffering through illness or disability has "bad" karma. The reverse may be true: that their suffering is a form of spiritual development.

Life on earth is not a holiday camp but a learning experience - a cement mixer in which individual souls with material bodies and free will interact with each other and the environment in an incredible free-for-all, with the overall aim of understanding themselves, the world and God. However a few decades in the cement mixer gives only a limited opportunity for development, and therefore the individual soul at some time after death is reincarnated into another body for another opportunity to progress on the spiritual path. This may carry on for many lifetimes, indeed indefinitely for those who make no progress. It is believed that success is finally achieved when the soul is completely enlightened and enters a state of God-realisation.

Life on earth can be illustrated by a story about a young man and a wise sage. The young man said "Sir, can you tell me if there is such a thing as Hell?" The wise sage replied, "Where do you think you are now?" In the Christian religion the icon of the crucified Jesus is used to demonstrate that religion is not about condemnation but empathises with the suffering experienced by so many in their lives.

Suffering is an inescapable part of spiritual evolution. We don't willingly choose to evolve until we are shocked into doing so by some form of suffering, be it physical, mental, emotional or spiritual. According to the doctrine of reincarnation, sin leads to greater suffering whereas right action, or righteousness, brings us closer to God; free will allows us to choose which path to follow. Unfortunately it is not immediately apparent to mortal humans which actions lead us into suffering; the great delusion of life that we have to deal with is the belief that happiness can be found by the indiscriminate satisfaction of our desires. So often we appreciate we are on the wrong road only when we find that we have been led into suffering by the thoughtless pursuit of sense pleasures or other ephemeral indulgencies. However the development process is self-regulating because if an individual is on a downward path, at some time they will come to the realization that there is another way, that they have the ability to choose a path that will lead them away from suffering. The principle of self-regulation is the basis of universal existence, and reincarnation extends this principle to the human species.

For many people God is the last thing to think of; it is only when they suffer and can find no other way of dealing with their problems that they pray to God for help. It is paradoxical that, in this way, suffering is a path to God. It seems that there is inevitability about humanity's relationship with God; either we choose, maybe with some assistance from others, to seek God or we are forced by our own or others suffering to ask God for help.

This scenario of life is accompanied by a sense of destiny. We are not like puppets but the principle of karma means that each person is likely to be presented with challenges and opportunities as a consequence of their past actions. Each person has a particular part to play in life's drama and if anyone overplays or underplays their part, the whole performance suffers. We are not given a script but have to ad lib as best we can, hoping that all will be well. We have to make decisions, which are sometimes momentous. We have to make judgements, about when to be tolerant, when to be compassionate, when to be critical, when to be assertive, when to be pacifying. We need guidance but don't always go to the best sources. An excellent source of guidance is a well-developed spiritual intuition. Another source is a spiritually-orientated code of conduct such as given by Patanjali.

Many people find it difficult to accept the idea of suffering in a world where there is a God. They ask, "Why does a benign God allow suffering?" The answer lies in the very nature of God. God, through His natural laws, has overseen the development of the universe; He is the architect and facilitator of the process but not the builder or the manager. Planet earth, while forming a very small part of this universe, has developed a relatively benign environment that has enabled life to form and to evolve to the present advanced state of humanity. It is not for humans to demand to be kept in a state of bucolic happiness. God should not be seen as a puppeteer and therefore be held responsible for the condition of humanity. In a sense mankind, as a species, has chosen to evolve here, and as gods-in-the-making are God's junior partners. Much of the suffering in the world is inflicted by humans on themselves or on other humans; much suffering is a result of delusive beliefs about the source of happiness. It is the responsibility of humans to learn how to live, how to live together and to learn the true source of happiness; they cannot do this while denying God's existence.

Reincarnation answers the obvious question: how can a human achieve their full potential within a single lifetime? The explanation for the achievements of great human beings – Mozart, Darwin, Gandhi, Einstein – must be that they have had many previous lives. Equally reincarnation offers the potential for the lowliest to achieve ultimate greatness.

The doctrine of reincarnation, the theory of evolution, righteousness and an ethical code complement each other. Reincarnation provides a process whereby human souls can evolve over many lifetimes; an ethical code is like a handrail which they can use to assist their upward progress. If they lose hold of the handrail they jeopardize that upward progress. An ethical code has significance both for the evolution of the human soul, and for the secular life of communities; the same ethical code facilitates both the spiritual development of the human soul and harmonious communal life. The sanction for obedience to the code of ethics is in part spiritual, in that an individual has to live with the consequences of his past actions; additionally there may be secular sanctions for cases where the law has been broken. The spiritual and secular sanctions reinforce each other.

Evolution theory explains the process whereby the amazing diversity of species currently existing on earth developed from a single organism; this is a systemic process with little conscious individual involvement. The theory of reincarnation explains the self-regulated spiritual development of individual souls. Reincarnation requires discrimination and judgement on the part of individuals to enable them to live righteously in the world and to achieve spiritual progress. It also requires discrimination and judgement on the part of society in applying rewards and sanctions to encourage individuals to live appropriately.

Suffering raises the challenging question of guidance and help for those in difficulty. Because of the interconnectedness of humanity it is incumbent on us to offer assistance to those who suffer, even though this help or guidance may be repulsed. This applies particularly to those who are easily led astray or those with limited resources who, once on a downward path are unable to change. It is tragic that so many young people drift onto a downward path as a result of an inadequate perception of the nature of life and its possibilities. Our educational system should include teaching on evolution, reincarnation, righteousness and a code of ethics to ensure that all young people grow up with an understanding of these essential matters.

It must be recognized that there is a conflict between the imperative to help those in need and one of the elements of evolution – survival of the fittest. There is a delicate balance between the Christian motivation to help those in need and self-preservation; a man who gives away all his wealth to the poor and ends up being dependant on others is not particularly righteous. The motives for helping others also need careful examination. Assistance given to others to assuage one's own disturbed feelings may be counterproductive if such assistance prevents the recipient learning from their mistakes.

The delicate balance is very evident at a societal level, where those motivated by Christian charity strongly advocate the provision of community (i.e. other peoples') resources to assist the many people in the world who are demonstrably in need. Leaders have the difficult task of ensuring that satisfying demands to help others through financial aid, humanitarian assistance, or enabling immigration does not endanger the national self-interest. Although it may be repugnant to Christians, the principle of evolution recognizes that more people are born on earth than can be supported and that some will, unfortunately, not survive. Britain, a country with about 1% of the earth's population, must preserve its own existence if it is to help the rest of the world. The best help it can give is advice which is in tune with the principles of evolution and righteousness. A later chapter deals with the problem of over-population.

The description of reincarnation given above is a hypothesis which may not satisfy those demanding a rigorous and scientific explanation. We do not know the medium that sustains the soul, or how the soul survives after the body's death. We do not know the way the soul in its incarnations is associated with its past experiences, its achievements and its mistakes. There have been instances of people who claim to remember previous incarnations, but for most of us birth into a fresh body without conscious remembrance is a good way to begin another chapter on our long journey to enlightenment.

One objection to the concept of reincarnation and a possible reason for its abandonment by the Christian Church is that many people like the idea fostered by the Church that at the end of their one life, regardless of their behaviour, they will have their sins forgiven and ascend to heaven. This comforting idea doesn't make sense.

Although the theory of reincarnation answers many questions, it also leaves some unanswered. Why are some people born with disability, even extreme disability? Why do some people who seem to have so much to live for, experience an early and tragic death? What explains the apparent accidental events that leave some people unscathed and others severely injured? Maybe even though reincarnation provides some rationality for our journey in life there is also randomness just as there is in the process of evolution. Some aspects of the world are governed by immutable laws while others – climate, earthquakes, volcanoes, tornados – demonstrate the unpredictability of life. One of the most unpredictable aspects is the whims and fancies that result from mankind's free will.

Despite the objections and remaining lack of definition, reincarnation, evolution, righteousness and an ethical code together provide a spiritual framework for a religion for the twenty first century. Humanity has reached the stage where – in partnership with God - it has the ability and the responsibility to take charge of its own development within the framework of such a religion.

Chapter 5

Orthodox Religion

The world is my country, all mankind are my brethren, and to do good is my religion.
Thomas Paine

Like many others I love Christian churches with their devotional atmosphere, and hymns with their inspiring music and uplifting words. These churches are a reminder of the faith that has inspired so many believers over the centuries. I recognize the enormous value that followers of religion receive from their faith, and the huge contribution to society made by these believers and the charitable infrastructure they support. However the huge crises that presently face us demonstrate failure on the part of Christian churches to inculcate the principles of righteousness in society.

Weakness of the Church

Religion can be said to serve four functions:

- It provides support and comfort during our life on earth.
- It explains the unknowns of human existence.
- It gives a promise that we will live after corporeal death.

- It provides rules to live by.

The Christian Church does very well on the first item, which includes pastoral support. Its theology is unconvincing for the next two items, and would be much improved by the adoption of the doctrine of reincarnation. It is the last item which has a huge impact on society and which I address here; rules refer to righteousness.

Religion is the guardian of the principle of righteousness, and the duty of religion to encourage society to be righteous is both a challenge and an opportunity; if religion doesn't do it no one else will. The task of religion is to nurture a culture that supports righteousness in society, whether in the thoughts and behaviour of ordinary people, of workers in every walk of life, of business leaders in boardrooms or of politicians in the Cabinet Room.

However religion does not have absolute power to impose what it regards as the principles of righteousness. Throughout history there has been tension between religion and rulers; even today in China tension between Buddhists and the state has resulted in violence. Wherever they are, rulers do not like to be told how to behave by those it regards as having no authority. In Britain today Christianity has been emasculated by the juggernaut of secularism. The message most commonly associated with Christianity – often seen on posters outside churches - is that 'GOD IS LOVE'. The secular music industry has amplified the message and embedded it deep in the nation's psyche with songs such as the Beatle's 'All you need is love, love'. Few Christians would deny the importance of love in personal relationships, but the over-simplicity of the message suggests that other divine characteristics are of little importance.

The central message 'God is Love' ignores characteristics that, I believe, are equally important, for example: truth, consciousness, awareness, wisdom, discrimination, determination, decisiveness, judgement. An exclusive emphasis on 'love' has resulted in a devaluation of these qualities that are important in both personal life and in the conduct of public affairs.

The myth that 'all you need is love' has conditioned the public to accept the rule of demagogues whose mandate of compassion, charity, and international brotherhood is simply a license for unrestrained egotism. Such institutional and indiscriminate kindness is closely associated with the Law of Unintended Consequences, by which acts intended to be helpful, only make things worse.

The illusion that 'all you need is love' leads to a wooly nihilistic belief that no particular thought or effort is needed to deal with life's problems, only love and its associated qualities compassion, charity and forgiveness. This in turn leads to a schizophrenic existence, with a mental construct of an ideal world where all problems can be solved by love, side-by-side with the real world where one is faced with the dire results of policies formulated to operate in the mental construct. This schizophrenia has grave results both in personal lives and in the conduct of the nation's affairs.

The most important spiritual principle advocated by any religion should be righteousness and its values which include truth, abstinence from violence, theft, and greed. In many ways the first quality – truth – is the most important because in today's complex world the absence of truth, for whatever reason, can seriously corrupt society. As I demonstrate in a later chapter, religion is failing to imbue society with righteousness with disastrous results. Christianity needs a second Reformation to enable it to perform its proper role in the world of today.

Religions are not perfect; it is in their nature to create institutions which have a profound belief in their own importance, are preoccupied with self-preservation and are unable to perceive the necessity for change. Humans are souls with divine associations but the institutions they create are simply organizational structures that have no divine significance. Faith-based institutions seem to develop an almost fanatical belief in the veracity of their own scriptures and an intolerance of alternative beliefs. Followers are encouraged, not to develop spiritual insights of their own, but to immerse themselves in centuries-old scriptures and to relate today's world to these ancient writings. This results in an introverted and blinkered approach to spirituality.

Faith-based institutions inevitably adopt teachings which enhance their own power. An example is the practice of "indulgencies" – the forgiveness of sins by the clergy in return for a donation from the sinner; this was based on the comfortable belief that the clergy, as agents of God, had the divine ability to forgive sins. This practice, obviously open to corruption, led to the Protestant Reformation nearly 500 years ago when Martin Luther objected to the practice of "indulgencies". The gradual abandonment of such practices left a vacuum in the Church's doctrine regarding how to deal with sin, and even to define and talk about it. The authority of the Church suffered a further blow with the publication of 'On the Origin of Species' in 1859 and the loss of belief in the inerrant nature of the Bible. The Church seems to have lost any sanction to deal with unrighteousness. Wider society has been seriously affected by this reluctance to offer guidance which has begun to seem inhibiting and old-fashioned.

Sin, as well as having religious implications, has considerable secular significance where it may be antisocial or even criminal. Society needs a way of dealing with sin beyond simply 'hating the sin but loving the sinner'. Unfortunately the faith-based ethical code that once supported British society has been replaced by moral relativism. References to 'sin' or 'righteousness' are seen as old-fashioned, out-dated, even offensive. 'Discrimination' has become something unacceptable. There has been a coarsening of society. There is a general erosion of conscience throughout society from the highest levels to the lowest: in personal relationships, in public behaviour, in corporate activity, in the conduct of public affairs. Untruthfulness in the form of 'economy with the truth' and 'spinning' is commonly tolerated. There is a failure to deal with crime in an appropriate way, a failure which derives from a deep spiritual malaise.

Another unfortunate habit of religions is to create mysteries which only their clergy seem to understand; this, of course, empowers the clergy and evokes unquestioning obedience from the ordinary believer. There is, inevitably, mystery associated with the nature of God. However I find it difficult, as a pragmatist, to accept the mysteries that religions create and which they expect us to accept at face value. Examples are the stories of Jesus' crucifixion and resurrection, the idea that humanity is redeemed by such sacrifice, and the concept of ever-lasting life for those (but only those) who believe in Jesus. Religion says that these stories have divine authority; that they have been revealed by God and therefore cannot be changed in any way. The attribution of some of the scriptures to God was probably justified by the need for religious leaders to invest these documents with divine authority, and so encourage acceptance by their followers. It is time to recognize that much of what was written in the scriptures was allegorical, because allegory is an excellent way to convey essential truths; nevertheless it is not literally true.

Religions need to come to terms with the scientific evidence about the true history of the world and to accept that different religions can worship God each in their own way and without persecuting others. One of the main problems with orthodox religions has been their evangelistic fervour, a belief that they alone are right, and a determination to convert others at any cost. Religions might attract a greater following if, instead of trying to convert people, they simply got on with their primary task of encouraging righteousness amongst individuals, businesses and particularly government.

Religion needs to become less introspective and more concerned with the secular world. This doesn't mean more bishops in the House of Lords, but that those with a faith should raise the standard of righteousness at every opportunity, ensuring that as far as possible the conduct of public affairs is carried out in a righteous manner. There are many precedents for political activity by those with spiritual beliefs. A fine example is William Wilberforce, a Christian, and a Member of Parliament for Yorkshire who was convinced – unsurprisingly - of the importance of religion, morality and education. He supported the campaign for a complete abolition of slavery which resulted in the Slavery Abolition Act of 1833. He died shortly after and was buried in Westminster Abbey. A more modern example, from the USA, is Martin Luther King, a Baptist

Minister and a leader of the civil rights movement. He led the 1963 civil rights march on Washington and received the Nobel Peace prize for his work to end racial discrimination through non-violent means including civil disobedience. Later chapters demonstrate that the crises facing Britain and the world are immense, and demand spiritual contributions from men and women of the calibre of Wilberforce and Luther King.

For religion to be more effective in public affairs, it needs a new spiritual framework to convince the public that religion is relevant in secular matters; that it deserves to be heard and that it can make a positive, even vital, contribution. Such a new framework is proposed in Chapter 11.

Christianity – the national religion

Christianity has been the national religion of Britain for centuries. Its values are the basis for our laws and legal system. Its churches operate throughout the country and offer extensive pastoral services. It plays a prominent part in local communities, in education and in significant national ceremonies. Its infrastructure makes an immense contribution to communal life.

In recent years the growth of large immigrant communities with their own religious affiliations have presented an apparent challenge to the presence of the Christian Church. This challenge is largely perceived by secular authorities who subscribe to the false god of "equality" and want to see an equal treatment of all religions. This demonstrates the ludicrousness of the idea of "equality". The champions of "equality" would either want to see priests of every religion present on every occasion when a religious presence was required (which would be ridiculous), or none (more likely). The principle of "equality" is used by secular authorities to justify the banning of Christian communal celebrations – such as Christmas – on the grounds that they are offensive to other faiths.

Christianity is the historic, primary religion in Britain, and should continue to be so. Most other religious faiths in Britain are happy with this state of affairs because they are happier that a faith of some sort should be represented in civic affairs than none at all. It has to be presumed that those who come to Britain do so because they have some admiration, even respect, for our way of life. They have a right, as any British citizen, to follow whatever faith they find appropriate. However it has to be accepted that Christianity is the national religion with various cultural implications.

Those who come to Britain as admirers of our way of life rather than as conquerors will not object.

Chapter 6

False Gods

Decadence can find agents only when it wears the mask of progress.
               George Bernard Shaw

False gods are a form of delusion. For the best of motives a principle may be elevated to a status that is god-like such that it is beyond question, beyond pragmatic consideration. Noble qualities such as compassion and charity can be distorted when applied unquestioningly; the road to hell is paved with good intentions. Elevation to a god-like status can also happen with less noble dogmas which invest followers with such absolute slavish conviction that they object violently to any questioning of their beliefs.

The first of the Ten Commandments is: "I am the Lord your God and you shall have no other gods before me." In many ways the importance of this commandment lies in its proscription of other, false, gods. Through breaking this commandment and creating false gods, leaders find it easy to break other commandments by reason of the claimed sanctity of these false gods and their demands.

Throughout history leaders have set themselves up as false gods and it has required many years of struggle to develop political systems whose aim is to restrain leaders and insist that they serve the ordinary people. Thus Britain prides itself on being a nation with a long history of democracy. However there has been a gradual increase in the extent of the state which now consumes almost half the nation's annual income. This income is needed to pay for defence, education, health, welfare, a large number of public employees, and a variety of goods and services. The size of the state, and the amount of legislation it produces, puts an enormous amount of power in the hands of the Government of the day. The success or failure of businesses is critically dependant on the level and form of taxation, and on legislation directed at business. There is no advantage to business in being antagonistic towards Government, and every advantage in being on good terms. Similar comments apply to the media and other institutions. This is a recipe for patronage, where bees gather round the honey pot of Government. In effect a Government can set itself up as a false god, above and beyond the requirements of righteousness, dispensing largesse to its favourites and rewarding those who extol it.

It is paradoxical that quasi-religious movements have been created by today's secular politicians who worship false gods. These ideologues, misusing powers given them by the electorate, create cults which worship at the shrine of pseudo-spiritual principles given the attributes of godliness. The creation of such false gods empowers their inventors who may even deny the existence of the true God. Cult followers respond, as if hypnotized, to words to which they have been sensitized. One example is "equality". Enter the word on Google and you will find some 29,000,000 entries (compared to 7,000,000 for "righteousness"). It is a very popular false god, but nothing to do with righteousness, and everything to do with fuelling feelings of envy and resentment among those who feel themselves unequal.

The doctrinaire application of "equality" was wonderfully satirized by George Orwell in *Animal Farm*, in which a group of animals, led by cunning pigs, revolt and take over their farm from a farmer who had mistreated them. They define seven commandments, the seventh and most important being: *All animals are equal.* By the end of the story, in which the pigs gradually corrupt the original fine ideals, only one commandment is left and that reads: *All animals are equal but some are more equal than others.* Nothing illustrates better the corruption of high ideals by the political process. The underlying truth of this satire is continually demonstrated in political life, where those elected on a platform of "equality" rapidly become (like Orwell's pigs) more equal than others.

When John F. Kennedy made his presidential inaugural address in 1961 and invited the people of the USA to "ask not what your country can do for you, ask what you can do for your country", he directed the attention of his listeners away from their own individual wants and instead towards the needs of the wider community. He encouraged each individual to expand their consciousness and consider the positive role they could play in their country, the contribution they could make to society; instead of confining their attention to the different ways in which each person felt in need of help from the community. His words point to the negativity of an obsessive pursuit of "equality".

Throughout history there have been calls from the downtrodden for fair treatment – why should some people live in luxury when others are starving? Why should a working man not receive a fair wage? The gradual evolution of this demand for fairness into demands for "equality" has seemed natural but is pernicious and subversive. It creates dissatisfaction and destroys cohesion by encouraging each person to search for ways in which they are being treated less than equally, instead of grasping whatever opportunities they are presented with and playing a rewarding part in the community.

Thomas Paine, who curiously died the same year Darwin was born, argued forcefully in *Rights of Man* for political rights for all men because of their natural equality in the sight of God. He is rightfully admired for his radicalism, but the "natural equality in the sight of God" that he championed was far removed from the artificial concepts of equality promulgated in today's society.

"Fairness", although an imprecise word, is easily understood and can be applied pragmatically in the everyday world. However to refer in a legalistic way to "equality" in regard to humans who are utterly diverse and obviously unequal is absurd! This diversity and inequality is apparent in every field of human activity, whether work, leisure, sport or human relationships. Diversity exists not only in obvious physical characteristics but in characteristics such as energy, determination, intelligence, perception, kindness, humility, arrogance, ambition, aspiration, self-discipline, ruthlessness. Diversity also applies to the unique conditions that affect each individual: their parents, their grandparents, the date and time of birth, the place of birth, liability to sickness, the opportunities they are presented with, their friends, their partners. The principles of diversity and inequality are a necessary part of the theory of evolution based on survival of the fittest and natural selection. They also result from the reincarnation process because the myriad souls on earth are all at different levels of spiritual development. Any attempt to equalize this diversity and compensate for differences, if it were possible, would be a never-ending task.

It may be reasonable to apply the word equality to humanity in a general sense, and consider equal treatment in the context of fairness, but any attempt to define the equality of humans by legislation is manifestly absurd, and can only result in endless disputation and an enormous expansion in the numbers of people employed at considerable expense – although with no useful output - in such disputation. It might be said that this preoccupation with "equality" is the zeitgeiste or spirit of the age; unfortunately it exemplifies the denial of reality that pervades our political culture and which, unless it is confronted, can only lead to disaster.

Wherever there are groups of people, whether couples, families, large organizations or society, the challenge is to manage the interaction of immense human diversity in a productive way. This cannot be done according to a formula based on a doctrinaire definition of "equality" but can only be done pragmatically with an appreciation of the unique qualities of each individual. This managed interaction cannot properly be a function of an outside body but is a function in which all play a part. Obviously the quality of this interaction depends on the ethical norms that operate in and underpin society, and it is the responsibility of those concerned with the health of society to nurture these ethical norms. The imposition of an artificial concept of "equality" inevitably leads to a loss of sensitivity in relationships: a mindless application of the formula by some and exploitation of the formula by others.

Institutional emphasis on "equality" causes each individual to selfishly examine their lives to find any way in which they might have reason to claim that they are being treated less than equally – whether by society, or their employer or anyone else. It provides a platform for political and pseudo-political organizations who claim to champion the rights of those who feel themselves to be treated less than equally. The consciousness of society is thus lowered from an unselfish consideration of the contribution that each individual can make to the common good, to a selfish preoccupation with how one person is getting less out of society than another.

Equality is a specific mathematical concept which is corrupted by the way the word is bandied about by those with political interests. The only authority established to decide on man's equality is the law, which after due process can decide that crime has rendered a man unequal and subject to punishment. Therefore it is deemed that all men are equal in the eyes of the law, before any guilt is established. The religious view is that all men are created equal. The significant word here is "created". Men may have been created equal, in the sense of soul equality, but their own actions render them unequal in various senses. The world of "equality" is the flat world referred to by Ronald Reagan where there is no discrimination between human qualities and behaviours (although some people are strangely more equal than others).

The concept of "equality" has no place in human relationships. Ask any woman looking for a husband whether all men are equal; the answer will be a short one. We like some people and dislike others, we enjoy the company of some people more than others, some people are more talented than others; this reflects the rich pattern of human life and is nothing to do with "equality" which has somehow become a quasi-religious concept of the secular world. The concept of "equality" is cosmetic; we need to accept the fact of inequality just as we accept the theory of evolution which is based on inequality.

It is the application of the false god of equality to gender that has resulted in the extraordinary belief that women and men are really the same, that it is only a matter of culture how they are perceived! Even the Pope has responded to this aberration. The difference between heterosexuality and homosexuality is discussed elsewhere.

Another false god has been created in the word "discrimination", which has some 39,000,000 entries on Google. Most of these entries are concerned with people who feel they have not been treated "equally" and have therefore been the subject of "discrimination". I do not deny the need to have some sense of equality or to have some sense of discrimination, but believe that in matters of human relationships we need a sense of proportion; that sense is absent in a world where only false gods are worshipped. An alternative version of a false god is the claim for religion itself as 'an agent of change' to justify particular societal changes; this demeans religion by making it a political football. There is nothing more radical than religion, but its fundamental purpose for which there is great need, must be the advancement of righteousness, not the touting of favourite political schemes. The future of society depends on recognizing the one supreme God as part of a spiritual framework that includes evolution, reincarnation, karma, an ethical code and righteousness; and casting false gods aside.

Chapter 7

Righteousness in Society

To see what is in front of one's nose needs a constant struggle.
George Orwell

Humanity is on an evolutionary journey in which the quality of righteousness is its greatest support. Life on earth is a battleground between the forces of righteousness and the forces of delusion. This is a battle for the soul of humanity. Never underestimate the forces of delusion which are devious, insidious, surreptitious, and unrelenting. Humans have the choice between these alternative forces, and the responsibility for the outcome. God may love, bless and inspire the forces of righteousness, but humans have to do the work. If, for whatever reason, they choose to avoid the conflict; the forces of delusion win.

Christianity has many facets, and at any one time some facets are more obvious than others. The once popular and inspiring hymn "Onward Christian soldiers, marching as to war" has become unfashionable and today Christianity is more about humility, meekness, compassion, understanding, love. However when the principles of Christianity are under attack what is needed is evangelism, not in the sense of persuading others to adopt Christianity, but to uphold righteousness at a time when society seems to be drowning in delusion.

Righteousness can only be exercised with a belief in the one true God, not in delusional false gods. The effectiveness of right action can then be enhanced with the qualities of pragmatism and enlightened self-interest.

In the Britain of today the state is all-pervasive and legislation has a significant effect on patterns of behaviour. People are increasingly told by authority what they can and cannot do, have lost the habit of deciding for themselves what is right and wrong and instead have developed the attitude "If I can, I will". This robotic behaviour is reflected amongst public employees who, subject to a culture of detailed "targets", have developed the pattern of "box ticking" instead of considering what is the right thing to do. In some parts of society the quality of life has deteriorated to a level that is superficial, casual, flippant, cynical.

Whatever the prevalence of unrighteous behaviour throughout society, the leaders of society have a particular responsibility and it is their behaviour that is especially important. In a faith-based society, leadership is recognized as a special role that requires those who lead, to behave in a righteous way and to lead their followers on a righteous path. In an increasingly secular society, the loss of faith has resulted in an acceptance that leadership can serve itself and its own doctrines rather than the people it leads; this is a denial of the responsibilities of leadership.

Leaders – in politics, business, the media, and religious institutions – have a dual role. They must first live in as righteous way as they can; secondly they set the standards of behaviour in society, by their own actions, by their decisions, by legislation and by their failure to condemn undesirable or unacceptable behavior. Ordinary folk respond to the environment created by their leaders; they may initially resist the temptation to engage in activities which may be damaging, but over a period of time, as more and more people indulge in these activities without any obvious penalty, and no one in authority warns of dangers, everyone joins in; this downward path represents a betrayal by society's leaders.

Leaders have different responsibilities with regard to righteousness. Those in government have executive powers in the democratic system and have huge responsibilities for the legislation they enact and the manner in which they exercise authority; these leaders create the secular framework to which the common man is expected to conform. Those in political opposition have the much more limited role of constructive opposition to ensure that government behaves in a righteous way and to make it very clear if the government fails to do so. Business leaders, who operate in the market economy, have a responsibility to ensure that their institutions operate in conformity with the conditions set by government, and in a righteous way. Media leaders have a responsibility to ensure that news and comment are presented in a righteous way i.e. truthfully, without spin. Religious leaders have a prime role as the custodians and advocates of the principles of righteousness; it is they who must be willing to hold the other leaders to account.

The need to behave righteously applies particularly in the political field where politicians compete aggressively for election to office with the real or implied promise to protect the interests of those they serve. If elected they have the whole machinery of the state at their command; that machinery exists to enable leaders to serve the public. Leaders have to realise that election to office is a privilege which gives them no rights except the right to serve the public. Leaders are not elected to office simply to embrace fashionable causes, to cultivate popularity and to enhance their own reputation. Leadership is about making righteous decisions that lead upwards on the evolutionary path. This may be difficult and unpopular and require courage. The greater the office, the greater the temptations of delusion: cultivation of special interest groups, buying popularity, the various forms of untruthfulness, unjustified optimism, Micawberism – the list is endless. There are many different ways of being unrighteous, but only one way of being righteous.

Politicians may dismiss criticism by claiming that it is inspired by their political opponents. However, decisions that specifically endanger the nation's well-being and lead it down an evolutionary blind alley is a betrayal of the nation and is unrighteous. The role of politicians is especially critical when the state is as powerful as it presently is.

There are many examples in today's society of unrighteous behaviour, both by individuals in the mass of society and by the leaders of this society. However the current crises demonstrate two prime areas of society that suffer from the effects of unrighteousness; they are democratic government and the market economy. Both democratic government and the market economy are supposed to serve the interests of the people, but they are demonstrably failing to do so.

Democratic government is supposed to be "of the people, by the people, for the people" but in Britain, electoral apathy shows the public cynicism towards a political establishment which seems to be primarily concerned with serving itself and its own false gods. The market economy is supposed to serve the interests of the people through the various agencies of commerce but recent events has shown that institutions of the market economy have become obsessed with their own false god – mammon; instead of being content to run an effective market economy that enables the world's productive systems to function, these institutions have become so obsessed with extracting wealth for themselves that they have endangered the whole system. "Ruinous" is not too extreme a word to apply to the present state of collapsing markets, bankrupt companies and rising unemployment. But government has a duty to regulate the market economy and therefore it must bear responsibility for recent events.

Religion is the primary focus of this book and when I began there was no intention to discuss politics. However I found that increasingly I struggled to resist mentioning it. I finally had to accept that an examination of righteousness in the secular world cannot avoid considering the actions of the present British Government.

In the following pages there are various criticisms of the way leaders, including the British Government, have abandoned the principles of right-eousness. This is demonstrated by issues that include the financial crisis, the moral crisis, the world population crisis and the oil crisis. These are not simply matters of political controversy, but areas of life of enormous significance where acceptable standards of truthfulness, honesty and integrity have been ignored, and humanity has been led down an evolutionary blind alley. These areas are examined below, not just to attribute blame, but to establish what has gone wrong and begin to define a right course of action. The difficulties that have been experienced so far from these crises are simply a wake-up call, an indication of the disasters that await the whole of humanity if we continue down an evolutionary cul de sac.

Financial Crisis

At the time of writing the world is experiencing a financial and economic crisis which some say is the worst in history; every day brings more bad news. The crisis, predicted by many people, is the result of years of credit-supported extravagance by individuals, corporations and governments. This was delusion on a grand scale! The financial crisis, its causes and consequences have been reported, examined, and analysed to an extraordinary degree and I do not attempt to add anything to these discussions but to establish a relationship between the crisis and a lack of righteousness on the part of those involved.

The crisis seems to have developed through a combination of ill-judged compassion, incompetent regulation of the banking sector and what some would see as the natural desire of those working in the financial business to make as much money as possible. Banking regulations have been relaxed partly to allow people with low incomes to get mortgages and partly through incompetence. On the one hand ordinary people jumped at the chance to get a place on the housing ladder. On the other people in the property and financial business jumped at the chance to make money out of the rocketing housing market; they devised a range of tempting mortgage offerings and financial instruments which disguised the fact that money was being lent to people who would, in all likelihood, be unable to repay it. The message was lend, lend, lend. For a short time everyone was happy: first-time buyers got houses, existing house owners benefited from escalating house prices, bankers received enormous bonuses and governments wallowed in the feel-good factor. Then the roof fell in.

As a result of the global banking breakdown, the world is now facing a crisis of unprecedented proportions. The International Monetary Fund warns that the world is experiencing a global recession and will contract for the first time since the Second World War. It forecasts that advanced economies will shrink by an average of 2% in 2009, but that Britain will suffer the worst recession of any advanced nation and shrink by 3.8% in 2009 and 0.2% in 2010.

In the UK a Labour Government came to power in May 1997 and since then the person with the greatest responsibility for financial and economic policy has been Gordon Brown, the present Prime Minister.   As Chancellor of the Exchequer for a decade Gordon Brown claimed that his regime was economically competent and fiscally prudent. "Prudence" was a word that was used repeatedly by Gordon Brown to describe his policies. He boasted of having abolished the boom and bust cycle, and claimed credit for a continuing growth in Gross Domestic Product.   He enjoyed the boom and unfortunately made no preparation for the bust.

Gordon Brown initiated "light touch" regulation of the banking sector by taking supervision of the banking industry away from the Bank of England and giving it to the newly-created Financial Services Authority. This transfer of responsibilities from the Bank of England to the new Financial Services Authority apparently left some areas of the banking system unsupervised and unregulated; Gordon Brown wanted to encourage the growth of the banking industry. The FSA was a paper tiger; any warnings it issued to banks were ignored and it had no powers to enforce them. The Bank of England was left with the task of setting the bank rate in relation to cost of living statistics; these official statistics curiously omitted housing so that rocketing house prices had no effect on their deliberations.

Sir Fred Goodwin, the now disgraced ex-chief executive of the Royal Bank of Scotland, was a friend of Gordon Brown, and was given a knighthood for services to banking in 2004. The fashion for "light touch" regulation of banking was followed in the US in 1999 when Bill Clinton repealed the Glass-Steagall Act that had been introduced to stiffen regulation of American banking after the Wall Street crash.

The scene was set for one of the biggest bubbles in financial history. Global investors – such as those from oil-rich countries - were looking for investment opportunities. Bankers fell over themselves to find investments for this relatively cheap money. Sub-prime mortgages offered a wonderful opportunity. There was aggressive lending by banks and building societies that in some cases reached 125% of the value of the property being used as collateral with few checks on the ability of borrowers to service loans! Bankers used leverage to increase their profits and devised complex arrangements to make the investments appear safe. Banking bonuses became so high, that the size of the bonus became the main motivation for financial deals. For some house owners the annual increase in the value of their house exceeded their occupational earnings, and enabled them to borrow even more. Unfortunately the banks had made the fundamental mistake of borrowing money on a short term basis and lending it on a long term basis; when lenders became nervous and wanted their money back everyone was in trouble.

In retrospect it can be seen that the apparent prosperity of which Gordon Brown boasted was based on an astonishing and unsustainable growth in private and public debt. The percentage of household income saved was more than 10% in 1997 but had fallen to 0.4% by 2008. At December 2008 British consumers had £53.1 billion worth of debt on credit cards – 2.5 times the level of 10 years ago. In 1980 the ratio of household debt to GDP was 30%; by 1987 it had risen to 57%; today it is 162%, greater than that of the USA which is 135%. Britain now has the biggest national debt in the developed world; it is forecast to rise to more than £1 trillion by 2013. It may take decades for the country's finances to recover.

An extreme example of this strange period, when many people were hypnotized by a belief in never-ending expansion, was 70 year-old Bernard Madoff in the US who has pleaded guilty to orchestrating the largest fraud in Wall Street history. He ran a $65 billion Ponzi scheme that took money from new investors to pay out high returns to existing investors. In fact he never invested the money with which he was entrusted, but was able to attract many gullible clients with the large returns he offered.

In Britain, the collapse of the banking industry is an illustration of the results of the delusion which has gripped so many people especially bankers and those who should regulate them. Northern Rock collapsed and has been nationalized; Bradford &Bingley part nationalized and part sold to Santander; HBOS, Lloyds and the Royal Bank of Scotland have received so much money from the state that they are almost entirely owned by the state. The history of the Royal Bank of Scotland is an example of the hubris of the banking industry. In 1998 when Goodwin joined the bank as deputy chief executive it was a modest high street bank in Scotland. Although without technical bank training and formal banking qualifications, by 2001 he was chief executive with global ambitions and a strategy of aggressive expansion primarily through acquisition. RBS became the world's largest company with assets of £1.9 trillion and the fifth largest company by stock market value. In 2008 it lent more than $9 billion in leveraged buyouts, more than double its nearest rival. There was a particular focus on the US, where subsidiaries included the Citizens Bank and RBS Greenwich Capital. The latter was said to have the largest trading floor in the world and those in charge earned up to $25million a year in cash bonuses. It seems that these US subsidiaries were heavily involved in sub-prime loans and by 2007/8 were suffering significant losses. RBS also led the expensive purchase of Dutch bank ABN AMRO in October 2007, which weakened its balance sheet. The bank liquidity crisis of October 2008 brought RBS to a state of collapse such that the loss for 2008 of £24.1 billion was the largest annual loss in UK corporate history. When the extent of RBS's problems were brought to the attention of the British Government Sir Fred Goodwin was forced to resign and take early retirement at the age of 50 with a pension worth £17million paying some £700,000 a year. The head of Citizens Bank, Larry Fish, retired in 2008 with a pension worth $27million which pays him $2.2million a year.

So how did such a situation develop? It can be argued that apparently clever people in government and in banking must have known what was happening, knew that the state of affairs was not sustainable, but out of delusion and for their own benefit encouraged ordinary people to believe that it was. If this financial crisis is indeed the worst in history, then those who led us into it are guilty of behaviour that can only be described as heinous. The people who borrowed 125% mortgages may have been foolish, but it is they who may lose their homes and their small stakes; it is those who encouraged them in this foolishness, and gained by it, who are culpable.

The financial crisis has already had many victims. Ordinary people who can least afford to lose money, and who prudently saved money and invested it in solid British companies have seen these investments decimated; their pensions have been endangered; some bank deposits have been lost; interest on savings has been reduced to insignificant levels. Some businesses have closed; many employees have lost their jobs. Unemployment has risen to 2 million and is predicted to rise much higher.

In contrast the atmosphere in the financial world is illustrated by a report in The Daily Telegraph, October 25th:

"Economists from the World Economic Forum have blamed "out-of-control" chief executives for treating its annual Davos summits like a luxury party rather than a serious conference. Klaus Schwab, executive chairman of the WEF, said he regretted not forcing Wall Street and City executives to listen to the worries of leading economists about the credit bubble over the last five years. Mr Schwab is now intent on returning the conference to its intellectual roots, based on the 1944 Bretton Woods forum that discussed rebuilding the global financial system after the Second World War.

"The partying crept in" the 70-year-old economist said, "We let it get out of control, and attention was taken away from the speed and complexity of how the world's challenges built up."

The annual conference, set in the tiny Swiss skiing town, is bankrolled by the big Wall Street and City firms. It is now famous for VIP partying, deal-making and schmoozing rather than the exchange of policy ideas, despite in recent years economists warning about global finacial systemic meltdown. One of the WEF's sessions three years ago was entitled, "Spotting the Next Bubble Before It Bursts", co-chaired by former executives of the nationalized mortgage lender Freddie Mac and investment bank Goldman Sachs. Last January's meeting was attended by 2000 business men and politicians, and 24 heads of state who signed up to 500 discussions during the conference. But WEF senior director Lee Howell said: "I often wonder how many members were actually listening to what was being said. I know the American financial community didn't show up in Davos to listen." He confirmed yesterday that the next January meeting will be held under the theme of "Shaping the Post-Crisis World".

Isn't this extraordinary; that business leaders, economists and politicians have been meeting year after year in Davos supposedly to discuss the state of the world's finances and yet have allowed the development of the worst financial crisis in the world's history? And Davos is only one of the innumerable junkets that have been held for our leaders.

So how do our political and financial leaders measure up against the standards of righteousness? A lack of truth and honesty for a start. There is a strong possibility of theft. There has been an abundance of greed. There is not much evidence of purity, contentment, discipline, study or awareness of the Divine. All-in-all a great example of the dangers of hubris and delusion. Isn't there a need to establish and nurture a culture of righteousness in the banking industry and those who oversee it?

Moral Crisis

The credit binge is a metaphor for the lowering of society's moral standards: people were tempted into borrowing too much, lenders were tempted by huge profits to be made, politicians were tempted by the easy life that this situation gave them and made no attempt to control it till it was too late. The people who benefited most from the whole exercise – the lenders and the politicians – deny that it was their fault! In a similar way moral standards are in decline because of the attractions of temporary and illusory pleasures, and the inability of those who should be responsible for moral standards to defend them. The hubris of society's determined pursuit of financial extravagance, culminating in the credit crunch and the worst financial crisis in history mirrors the pursuit of moral indulgence.

Family life is central to the concept of righteousness since the birth, raising and education of children – who represent the future – must be an essential preoccupation for any society. Evidence of our society's debasement of moral standards is the loss of a sense of the sacred. An area of life that has, throughout history, been considered sacred is the duality of feminine and masculine, the process of sexual attraction, sexual union, procreation and the raising of children. Now, the perception of sex simply as a sense pleasure has lead to mindless sexual activity, promiscuity, and even the approval by the state of the perverse corruption of the sexual act – homosexuality – and its treatment by the state as equivalent to the union of female and male. Thus all activities have been brought down to the same level of triviality. Abortion – the killing of unborn children – is carried out mechanically as though pregnancy was simply an irritating inconvenience; there are more than 210,000 abortions in Britain every year, 99% of which are for social reasons. Young people are becoming involved in sexual activities at a younger and younger age.

Britain's rate of teenage pregnancy is the highest in Europe. It is proposed that girls as young as 13 will be urged to have contraceptive injections under government plans to reduce teenage pregnancy rates. The rates of sexually transmitted diseases are described as "rampant" and "frightening". Just as the bankers said that 125% mortgages were sustainable, so the apologists for this moral relativity claim that everything will be alright if children are taught at an earlier and earlier age about the mechanics of sex and the use of condoms.

The effect on society of this debasement of moral standards is corrosive: breakdown of relationships, fragmentation of families, lack of parental responsibility, poverty, children with low aspirations and low achievements, leading to crime, drugs, violence. Mr Justice Coleridge, a Family Division judge told a conference of family lawyers in Brighton recently that family life is in meltdown: "What is certain is that almost all of society's social ills can be traced directly to the collapse of the family life." He told delegates that family breakdown is as serious as economic decline, terrorism and street crime in terms of its threat to British society and is "on a scale, depth and breadth which few of us could have imagined even a decade ago". "I am not saying every broken family produces dysfunctional children, but I am saying that almost every dysfunctional child is the product of a broken family." An inquiry for the Children's Society reports that children living with lone parents or step parents are three times more likely to have behavioural problems as those living with married parents; that a third of 16 year olds live apart from their fathers.

Not surprisingly, religions support some kind of permanent union or marriage between man and woman to provide a stable basis for raising children, for containing the powerful sex drive with which man (and other animals) are endowed, for creating the basis for an orderly and creative society, and for providing a framework within which the complementary natures of men and women can develop. Such a union can be described as righteous and provides a framework within which the attributes of righteousness can be nourished. For centuries, throughout the world, marriage has played a central role in society and this special, sacred fundamental role has been recognized by the state and given a legislative framework.

Therefore the way in which the British Government has devalued marriage over the past decade is certainly not righteous and can only be described as sinful. Marriage has been devalued by encouraging cohabitation rather than marriage (through the tax and benefit system), by encouraging single-parenting by never-married mothers (even school children), and by - through legislation - elevating homosexual cohabitation to the same status as heterosexual marriage. All this has been justified on the grounds of 'equality' and 'non-discrimination'.

It is not my purpose to gratuitously criticize people for the way they live; people are free to choose how they live as long as they do not impose burdens on others. However by using state recognition to raise the status of some lifestyles, the Government has made those lifestyles a subject of public concern. This makes it necessary, in the public interest, to examine the righteousness of these lifestyles to determine to what extent they should be encouraged by a Government. It is sometimes said that new social legislation simply represents the way society is changing; this is a devious and misleading excuse. Legislation that enshrines a lowering of standards encourages an ongoing trend of falling standards.

The use of the principle of 'equality' is a double-edged sword. Since 'equality' has been brought into the argument, it has to be justified. Equality is a mathematical concept meaning that things are equal or the same. Objects can only be equal in terms of some quality: an orange can be considered equal to an apple in terms of their weight, their volume or the fact that they are both fruit, but everyone knows they are different. Similarly unrighteous behaviour is not equal to righteous behaviour. This is not about making critical judgements but recognizing that righteous behaviour is best for individuals and for the community, and should be encouraged rather than discouraged. Encouraging behaviour that causes suffering is not compassion but unrighteousness.

Therefore cohabitation is not equal to marriage and should be discouraged, single-parenting by never-married mothers is not equal to marriage and should be discouraged, and homosexual activity is not equal to heterosexual activity and should be discouraged. The only way to discourage unrighteous behaviour is to make it unrewarding.

It is no surprise that man's powerful sex drive, coupled with his ingenuity and curiosity has resulted over the years in many experiments with his sexual apparatus. This does not mean these experiments have any validity. Among the vast range of qualities possessed by humans is that of perversity, to a greater or lesser extent. Humans sometimes behave in ways that may seem unexpected, illogical, even against their best interests. Some people seem to behave consistently in this way. Homosexuality is an example of such perversity. Homosexuality is a perverse way of expressing sexuality, uses the body in unnatural ways, is barren, damages health, causes disease, reduces life span, imposes an unnecessary burden on the health service and is involved in anti-social activities such as 'cottaging'. Obviously, homosexuality represents an evolutionary dead end. Additionally, in single-sex establishments it can lead to bullying, seduction and rape. Within living memory in Britain homosexuality was considered sufficiently unrighteous to be an unlawful activity, incurring severe penalties. The first change to this situation was legislation to allow homosexual acts between consenting adults. This was generally accepted on the basis that while homosexuality is unrighteous, so is much of human behaviour. Unrighteous behaviour should not necessarily be identified as a criminal activity but neither should it be admired or encouraged. However, under intense pressure from vocal homosexual activists, representing a small proportion of the electorate, in the last decade Government legislation has enshrined homosexuality as equivalent to heterosexuality in every way including the teaching of its equivalence in schools, and allowing the adoption of children by homosexual men!

As argued above, a heterosexual man and a homosexual man may be equal in terms of weight, volume and both being humans and having souls; but they are completely different in that heterosexuality – part of the evolutionary scenario - provides a foundation for our continuing civilization and as such is righteous whereas homosexuality is unrighteous and should therefore be discouraged. There is no equality between heterosexual practice and homosexual practice, and a society that says they are 'equal', and legitimises this false 'equality' with the full force of the law, thereby encourages unrighteousness and falls into corruption and decadence. However the laws that have been passed in the last decade seek to ensure that homosexuals are treated 'equally' in all respects, thus making ordinary members of the public who object, liable to accusations of 'discrimination' or 'harassment' punishable by the full weight of the law. One might have expected the introduction of these laws to have been opposed adamantly by those with some appreciation of the importance of righteousness, but the churches are so weak or have been so intimidated by political correctness that they no longer have the stomach to defend the principle of righteousness.

Government's attack on marriage typifies its indifference to righteousness, an indifference that has been exhibited in other areas. A review of Britain's record for righteousness reveals a very sad state of affairs. Britain is now a world leader in family breakdown with the highest level of divorce and lone parenting in Europe. A report from Unicef, the UN's children's fund, points to statistical evidence that links growing up in single-parent families and step-families with a greater risk of dropping out of school, leaving home early, poorer health, low skills and low pay. Children from fractured families are more liable to behavioural problems, low educational attainments, low aspirations, drug taking and crime. Crime is increasing and the Home Secretary has had to ask judges to stop sending criminals to prison because they are so full. The Government extended the opening hours of licensed premises, to encourage a continental-style drinking culture; the result, which some predicted, has been an increase in drunkenness, and in alcohol-fuelled violence. Decline in the quality of radio and television broadcasting is well demonstrated by the volume and sordidness of swearing.

At the time of writing, moral standards in Britain are set on a downward path that can only be described as an evolutionary blind alley, because the values of our civilization are unsustainable in such a nihilistic society.

World Population Crisis

Population is a global problem and can only be dealt with through the coordinated actions of individual nations. The world is already experiencing the climactic effect of the financial bubble but has yet to experience the full effect of the population bubble. Warnings of the consequences of world population growth have been given by a variety of far-sighted individuals; in the UK the Optimum Population Trust is the only group now campaigning on population issues. There is nothing hypothetical about world population growth. The world's population, currently 6.8 billion, is heading for at least 9.2 billion by 2050. Even now many of the world's population are living in terrible conditions because the earth does not have sufficient resources to sustain them. It is estimated that the earth has the biological resources to sustain only 5 billion people. If all the world's population had a standard of living similar to that in developed countries, the earth would be able to support much less than this 5 billion.

For the UK, an urbanized, high-consuming nation with low self-sufficiency, the position is starker; currently we have a population of 61 million, but the resources to support only 17 million at the standard of life we currently enjoy! A United Nations report says that the UK population will rise to 72.4 million by 2050 including the yearly arrival of 174,000 immigrants. Shouldn't alarm bells ring?

World population has, throughout history, been limited by poverty, starvation, water shortage and conflict, and until the industrial revolution was less than 1 billion. The rapid rise of world population from 1 billion in the mid-19th century to the present level has been enabled by the availability of cheap oil with its enormous benefits – cheap energy, farm machinery, fertilizers, motorized transport, electricity, air transport, oil-based industry, and a higher quality of life - as discussed in the next section.

Throughout the world an expanding population forces people to spread to less hospitable areas: less productive, more environmentally hostile, more prone to conflict with others. Greater density of population creates stress. The media is constantly full of news about the latest conflict, the latest humanitarian disaster, the latest outbreak of disease, the intense poverty in the latest refugee camp. Yet extraordinarily our politicians seem unable to draw the obvious conclusion: humanitarian disasters are caused generally by over-population and the world needs to control its population. The situation represents the paradox that providing medical treatment to reduce disease, providing more food to reduce starvation, providing resources to alleviate poverty, and reducing the amount of conflict; results in an increased population that is even more susceptible to starvation, disease, poverty and conflict on an even bigger scale. Lifetime fertility statistics give values of 2.6 children per woman worldwide, 3.2 in developing countries excluding China, 4.7 in the less developed countries, and 5.4 in sub-Saharan Africa. These figures give some explanation for the constant humanitarian disasters in developing countries and demonstrate that it is impossible to deal with such disasters without addressing population. It is the increasing world population which has the primary responsibility for the increasing pollution of the planet and the increasing exhaustion of its resources. It is ludicrous to attempt to deal with these matters without confronting the source of the problem: population growth.

The answer to the world population crisis is simple, although not easy: a world population policy can only be based on encouraging women to have fewer children rather than encouraging them to have more. This would apply particularly in areas of the world that have a very high birth rate – which very often are the areas least able to support an expanding population. Such a policy would be achieved through a range of contraceptive techniques; the provision of international aid would be dependent on education programmes aimed at the adoption of contraception techniques.

Increasing population is a global problem that is a massive demonstration of the human collective liability to delusion: the sexual imperative results in conception and childbirth without any thought of how the resulting extra population will be supported, apart from a Micawberish belief that something will turn up. However the adoption of a world population policy is not the responsibility of individuals but of nations and their leaders. Unfortunately there is no indication that world leaders are giving any consideration to limiting population.

To deny that the world is overpopulated is dishonest; so why do our leaders avoid the problem? The time frame for most leaders is short; maybe a lifetime, maybe the time to the next general election.

They are not generally interested in intangible matters - such as quality of life – until the electorate forces them to consider it. It is in the nature of politicians to want power, and the more the better. The larger a nation's population, the more taxes the politicians can raise, and the more power they have. An increasing population results in greater economic strength which enables a nation's politicians to have a greater role on the world stage. Politicians are in the grip of a web of delusion which promises that happiness, and electoral success, can be found through an increasing population and an increasing Gross Domestic Product, ignoring the fact that increasing population density reduces the quality of life and stores up problems for the future.

Professor John Bligh in his book '*The Fatal Inheritance*' writes: "Sooner or later, mankind will have to face up to the reality of the situation in which it is placing itself. If it has not already done so, it will be forced to take the only possible action to prevent widespread starvation, uncontrollable pandemic disease, and genocidal conflicts of unprecedented magnitude. That is, of course, population control."

How harsh must the scourges of starvation, disease, poverty and conflict become before the world's leaders act to limit population? The UK is one of the world's most densely populated countries and apparently is set to become even more so as a result of immigration yet our leaders seem blind to the problem.

Oil Crisis

Oil and gas are fossil fuels that take millions of years to form. Since the first oil well was drilled in the mid 19th century, the planet's store of oil, built up over millions of years, has been used at a profligate rate to provide cheap energy for the world, and particularly for the USA and other developed countries. Oil has enormous benefits: it is easy to transport, it's full of energy and it can be refined into a variety of different fuels (diesel, petrol, kerosene) which can be used in many different ways. Oil has been complemented by electricity; fossil fuels enable us to produce electricity easily and cheaply. The special qualities of electricity have enabled us to use it to power a vast number of devices – ranging from industrial machinery to television sets. It is clean and enormously convenient. Much of our modern lifestyle (including industrial products such as plastics) is dependant on a steady supply of oil, gas and electricity. For the last 100 years or so we have had the joy of using a virtually free energy source; all we had to do was take it out of the ground. The energy in a gallon of petrol is about the same as the energy expended by a man working hard for a month. Finding oil – with its latent energy – has been the equivalent of a mass lottery win.

Unfortunately the earth's reserves of oil will not last for ever. When an oil well is first drilled getting oil is easy. At some point the pressure drops and the rest of the oil is harder and harder to extract. The point at which the oil starts to run out is the 'peak' for that individual oil field. Colin Campbell, founder of the international Association for the Study of Peak Oil and Gas, has defined peak oil as "the maximum rate of the production of oil in any area under consideration, recognizing that it is a finite natural resource, subject to depletion." ASPO's mission is to "define and evaluate the world's endowment of oil and gas; to model depletion taking due account of demand, economics, technology and politics; and to raise awareness of the serious consequences for Mankind."

In 1956 when a Shell geologist predicted that oil production in the USA would peak around 1970 everyone laughed, but in 1971 oil wells throughout Texas started to dry up. American oil production turned down and never recovered; ever since America has relied on foreign oil imports and securing these imports has dominated American foreign policy. The oil production in other countries has also peaked including Venezuela in 1970, Nigeria in 1979. The Shell geologist also predicted that the peak of global world production would occur at the end of the 20th century or early in the 21st century. It is significant that discovery of new oil fields is on a downward trend. The peak year for discovery was 1964; despite prodigious efforts oil exploration companies have never again found as much as they did in 1964, and the fields they discover get smaller and more costly to extract a given amount of oil. No major new oil fields have been discovered for twenty years. The result is that combined global oil and gas reserves have fallen dramatically from a peak in the 1960s and 1970s. For the last twenty years more energy has been produced each year but the amount of energy consumed to obtain that energy has increased more rapidly.

It is believed that the production of all oils will peak in 2011, and that all hydrocarbons including gas will peak about 2012.

Despite the very obvious fact that oil - formed over a period of millions of years – has been almost depleted within a relatively short time of 200 years, the earth's population expects to carry on consuming it at an increasing rate. The population of the developing countries – China, India etc – wishes to use oil to raise their living standards the same way as those in the West have already done. The world is confronted by a dislocation between a falling oil production and a growing demand, the dire result of which can only be imagined: certainly significant price increase, but ultimately conflict in one form or another. One laughable reaction of the world's politicians to this looming problem is biofuels. The main attraction of biofuels is for the large agricultural corporations who receive huge subsidies to grow the crops that are processed into biofuels. The disadvantage for the world's population is the reduction in land available to grow food crops, and the consequent increase in food prices, which is already apparent. Additionally there is some evidence that biofuels may be worse pollutants than oil. Biofuels will not solve the shortfall in oil. Another laughable reaction is wind power for which the main attraction is the large subsidy paid to manufacturers and installers of wind farms.

Nuclear energy may be a more appropriate way to deal with the shortage of oil and gas than rather than biofuels and wind energy. Other countries have been increasing the amount of electricity they obtain from nuclear power. The amount of electricity generated from nuclear power is 79% in France, 31% in Germany, 30% in Japan, 20% in Britain. Britain is woefully unprepared for the consequences of oil shortages. The 12 nuclear power plants operating in Britain are old and have outlived their 20-25 year life expectancy; governments have done nothing effectively to replace them.

It has been suggested that the increasing shortage of oil will lead to the death of 5 billion people. This prediction is in tune with reports from the Optimum Population Trust that the present world population of over 6 billion is unsustainable; that the rapid rise of world population from 1 billion in the mid-19th century to the present level has been facilitated by the availability of cheap oil and its associated benefits.

When oil production begins to fall, it may fall very quickly. Significant increases in the price of oil, as a result of shortage, will cripple the world's economies. The result of a severe shortage of oil will be truly apocalyptic: a return to the state of societies in the mid-19th century would be accompanied by devastation, chaos and misery as 5 billion people die from hunger, cold, disease, lack of water, warfare, civil conflict.

Unfortunately our leaders seem to be giving as little attention to the crisis of oil/gas supply as they give to the moral crisis and the world population crisis. This suggests that the conduct of our country's affairs need to be approached on a deeper level than sheer political expediency, and that some way should be found to express the principles of right action in the governance of Britain.

Chapter 8

Religion for the Common Man

My religion consists of a humble admiration of the illimitable superior spirit who reveals himself in the slight details we are able to perceive with our frail and feeble mind.
Albert Einstein

In 1942 Henry Wallace, an American Vice-President, predicted that the coming century would be the century of the common man. In many ways the lot of the common man throughout the world has improved since then, but there are also omissions in these improvements. In the developed world material improvements have taken precedence, while in much of the developing world despotism or anarchy still prevails or has even worsened. Throughout the world spirituality seems to have lost its way, which is tragic for the common man who has always found support, guidance, comfort and solace in religion whether primitive or sophisticated. If we are living in the century of the common man, it is reasonable for him/her to expect that spirituality should be expressed through a standard of righteousness supported by a code of ethics. This requires a reform of religion to ensure that it can uphold and promote righteousness - right action – throughout society and its various institutions.

This is a massive task.

We have to recognize various unpleasant facts about the condition of our society. The social environment to which we are exposed contains an ever-reducing content of ethical or religious matter. We are surrounded by, or surround ourselves with, a variety of entertainments and amusements – television, computer games, celebrity mania – that inhibit consideration of ethical matters. This may not have happened as a result of conscious decision, but it will need conscious decision and resolute determination to change it. The shape of society has developed under the influence of secular forces that together represent a juggernaut that simply ignores ethical considerations. The only posssible challenge to this juggernaut is from a reformed, revitalized, vibrant religion.

Certain major functions of civilization such as democracy and the market economy have evolved to a condition that may appear sophisticated to people from past times, but which is still rudimentary. Henry Wallace said that "Democracy is the only true political expression of Christianity" but it is obvious from recent history that both democracy and the market economy are failing the common man. Politicians have learnt how to exploit democracy for their own advantage; business leaders have similarly learned how to manipulate the market economy to serve themselves. Both democracy and the market economy play an essential part in civilization but their further evolution depends on the extent to which righteousness can be brought to bear on their operation. The only institution that can promote and uphold righteousness throughout the various activities in the world is religion - updated for the twenty first century.

The principle of evolution applies to humans' understanding of God as well as to humanity itself. The nature of God as understood by humans today is very different from the understanding centuries or millennia ago. It is unfortunate that the religious model that suited that ancient understanding has not evolved and is no longer appropriate. An institutional model of a church empowered by the word of God, whose priests transmit the commandments and teachings of God to his worshipers, and act as intermediaries, does not work in today's world. The dichotomy between humans' understanding of God and the theology offered by the church has resulted in a growing atheism.

The maturity, understanding and sophistication of modern humans means that they will not blindly follow commandments supposedly issued by God and overseen by religious priests. They have free will to choose how they behave and need a convincing explanation of the advantages of righteousness and the penalties for unrighteousness. However they may accept a pragmatic code of ethics supported by the sanctions of karma and reincarnation, which ensure that the consequences of actions cannot be avoided. This empowers religions which advocate righteousness as both a spiritual and a secular quality; and promote an understanding of reincarnation and karma.

If the common man is advised to follow an ethical code, he is entitled to expect that religion will make the same demands of businesses operating as part of the market economy, and of government and the political system. As I have shown earlier both the business world and the political world have a deep need for encouragement to practice righteousness. This creates a challenge for religion; it is one thing to advocate righteousness to humble citizens who are committed believers, and quite another to challenge very powerful people who are intent on a short term course of action for their own advantage. However it should be seen as part of the evolutionary process of religion, of democracy and of the market economy that religion should be closely involved in the ethical standards of these two essential parts of modern civilization.

I suggest that the following precepts could be used as a basis for reformed religion – particularly Christianity – in the twenty first century:

- Biblical scripture is historical text, written by humans, and is open to interpretation by humans.
- There is one supreme God worshipped by many religions in different ways.
- The theory of evolution, proposed originally by Darwin, is fully accepted.
- The age of the earth is over 4 billion years.
- The doctrine of reincarnation defines the proper path for spiritual advancement and ultimately reunion with God.
- The concept of karma provides a compelling incentive for right action.
- Righteousness represents an aspirational standard of behaviour to support spiritual development and harmonious temporal life.
- An ethical code, such as that defined by Patanjali, provides a basis for righteousness.
- Democracy is the only true political expression of Christianity.
- One of the main responsibilities of religion is to promote righteousness in all aspects of life.
- Beware of false gods.

The present state of Christianity in Britain reflects the weakness of its underlying theology. For most Christians the religion is temporal, concerned with guidance for living according to Christian values but with little sense of spirituality or an afterlife. For many people the guiding rules are: "You only live once" and "You're a long time dead". There seems to be no effective spiritual sanction to encourage anyone to behave in a righteous way or to seek God.

Reincarnation is a pragmatic and convincing concept that it is well understood, was once accepted by early Christians and has been revered in the East for many years. Reincarnation is accompanied by the concept of karma: the fact that no one – individuals or nations - can avoid the consequences of their actions. Together, reincarnation and karma offer a sanction to encourage righteousness. The adoption of the doctrine of reincarnation by Christianity would reinvigorate the religion and enable it to play a much more effective part in the affairs of the nation.

These changes would be accompanied with the acceptance that all religions worship the same God but in a variety of forms to reflect a range of differences: cultural, tribal, time of origin. Nevertheless it will be recognized that a nation needs a national religion to reflect its history and culture and as a basis for its laws, its values, its public ceremony and a framework for education. In Britain the national religion is Christianity, although all people are free to worship as they choose.

The need for religion to play an effective part in British life is greater than it ever was. The state is more powerful than it ever was, operates within a political regime of doubtful integrity and needs to be brought under the control of a democratic system. The forces of the market economy are more powerful than ever and also need to be more effectively regulated. Only a spiritual authority, operating on behalf of the common man, has the capability to shine the spotlight of righteousness on these vital areas of human life and to strengthen the expectations of ordinary people that righteousness will form a major element in the conduct of political and business affairs.

Humanity's greatest challenge is its sheer diversity: in race, gender, manner of life, quality of life, language, dialect, accent, national affiliation, culture, custom, physical ability, mental ability, state of health, and appearance, not to mention the immense differences in personality that can even create problems within one family. This diversity is often divisive. There is only one unifying factor on which humanity can rely: God. This is illustrated by the greeting commonly used between people in India and South-East Asia known as "Namaste", which is derived from Sanscrit, and can be translated as "I greet the God within". The greeting is a recognition that within each person there resides some aspect of God – sometimes known as the Self or the Buddha-nature. The greeting emphasizes the soul-equality of humans and their resulting inter-connectedness. Soul-equality is completely different from the shallow concept of secular equality that causes so much confusion. An appreciation of soul-equality helps to assuage the resentments that arise from an obsessive preoccupation with the conditions of earthly existence and raises the consciousness above concerns of the transient material world. It brings a reverential quality to relationships, that reduces the significance of material differences.

Chapter 9

Conclusions

It is not the strongest of the species that survives, nor the most intelligent, but the one most responsive to change.
                                                    Charles Darwin

The following arguments have been presented:

- Humanity is on an evolutionary journey; women and men are gods in the making and have a vital part to play in this evolutionary process.

- Humanity is presently threatened by a range of issues which are potentially apocalyptic. This is a wake-up call that demands a radical response.

- The cause of major problems in the world can be identified as a lack of righteousness on the part of our leaders.

- Righteousness is a quality that has been neglected by society and has become unfashionable. Throughout history it has underpinned civilized life; its decline represents a failure of religion whose duty as a custodian of righteousness is to encourage and nurture it.

- Religions have not adapted to humanity's changing understanding. Christianity needs reform to provide sanctions against unrighteous behaviour. Such a sanction is available from the doctrine of reincarnation.

- Righteous behaviour is not only brought about by sanctions, but by prayer. Those with faith have the ability to seek God's blessing and guidance even for those without faith.

- Evolution, reincarnation and righteousness are the main principles of a religion for the twenty first century.

- The great diversity of humanity represents a need for the unifying influence of God.

Further Reading

THE HOLY BIBLE, Authorised King James Version.

THE BHAGAVAD GITA, translated from the Sanskrit with an introduction by Juan Mascaro, Penguin Books.

HOW TO KNOW GOD – THE APHORISMS OF PATANJALI, translated by Swami Prabhavananda and Christopher Isherwood, Vedanta Press.

Charles Darwin, *On the Origin of Species*.

Paramahansa Yogananda, *AUTOBIOGRAPHY OF A YOGI*, Self-Realization Fellowship.

Paramahansa Yogananda, *THE YOGA OF THE BHAGAVAD GITA*, Self-Realization Fellowship.

Paramahansa Yogananda, *MAN'S ETERNAL QUEST*, Self-Realization Fellowship.

Henry A. Wallace, *The Century of the Common Man*, Reynal & Hitchcock.

Professor John Bligh, *The Fatal Inheritance*, Athena Press.

Vernon Coleman, *Oil Apocalypse*, Blue Books.

Bart D Ehrman, *Misquoting Jesus*, HarperOne.

Jeffrey Satinover, MD, *Homosexuality and the Politics of Truth*, Baker Book House.

George Orwell, *Animal Farm*.

George Orwell, *Nineteen Eighty-Four*.

David Selbourne, THE PRINCIPLE OF DUTY, Sinclair-Stevenson

Roberto Assagioli, *Psychosynthesis*, Turnstone Press.